"When do you decide you are a successful parent? When your child is sixteen? Hardly. As Proverbs 22:6 says, 'Train up a child in the way he should go: and when he is old, he will not depart from it.' Sixteen is not old enough. Let's try forty. Here's my rule of parental perspective: decide how good a parent you are when your child becomes forty."

With scriptural backup, Dr. Kilgore certainly offers some comforting news to all parents!

Dr. Kilgore's Feel Good Parenting Book will help you to be less judgmental about your parenting skills and will enable you to view parenthood long-range so you can:
- *prepare for the stresses of raising children*
- *pass your values on to your children*
- *establish priorities within your family*
- *ground your family's faith*
- *renew your post-parental marriage*

Dr. Kilgore's FEEL GOOD Parenting Book

James E. Kilgore

Power Books

Fleming H. Revell Company
Old Tappan, New Jersey

TO Joy,
my daughter,
whose uniqueness has sometimes caused me to fear,
occasionally driven me to tears,
but much more often brought a smile of pride.

Unless otherwise noted, Scripture quotations are from the King James Version of the Bible.

Scripture quotations identified TLB are taken from *The Living Bible*, Copyright © 1971 by Tyndale House Publishers, Wheaton, Ill. Used by permission.

Library of Congress Cataloging-in-Publication Data

Kilgore, James E.
    Dr. Kilgore's feel good parenting book.

    1. Parenting—United States. 2. Parents—
United States—Religious life. I. Title.
II. Title: Feel good parenting book.
HQ755.8.K55   1986   659.1   86-15585
ISBN 0-8007-5297-X

Copyright © 1986 by James E. Kilgore
Published by the Fleming H. Revell Company
Old Tappan, New Jersey 07675
Printed in the United States of America

Contents

PART FOUR:
PARENTING PROFITS

Introduction

On a radio call-in program not long ago, a harried parent expressed frustration through a slogan: *Insanity is hereditary; you get it from your children.* Perhaps that type of stress, even if comically expressed, really explains why I chose to write this book.

I've read a number of books about raising responsible children that left me feeling guilty as a parent. I hope this book leaves some parents feeling good about themselves and what they are doing with their children. I believe that is the hope of our children. I've learned that through thirty-two years of ministry and eighteen years as a marriage and family therapist.

When parents feel good about themselves, and when their children see their marriage commitment is strong, those children grow up healthy and well adjusted. They in turn become good parents. Seeing families move toward positive mental health has been my greatest reward as a therapist.

If, as a parent, you can maintain your own mental health while your children grow up, you'll survive, and they will love you for it. Here's hoping the ideas in the pages that follow give you some new satisfactions in your pursuit of the parenting responsibility.

PART ONE

Parenting Perspective

"A happy family is but an earlier heaven."

John Bowring

ONE

The Promise
of Parenting

"The family is one of nature's masterpieces."
George Santayana

The Bible makes a promise to parents: "Train up a child in the way he should go: and when he is old, he will not depart from it" (Proverbs 22:6).

When I read those words, I see fulfilled parents, happy children, and peaceful lives. They do exist, but since I'm a marriage and family therapist, I meet far more parents who are distressed, discouraged, even defeated about their relationships with their children.

When Norman and Cynthia telephoned for an appointment, the problem they wanted to deal with was their marriage. Forty-five minutes into their first visit, I realized most of their talk had been about the frustrations of parenting.

Norman was a "man's man." A middle manager with a major national firm, he wore his dark suit, white shirt, and red striped tie handsomely, but without real comfort. "Would you believe I got a promotion when I started wearing suits to the office?" he asked. "I don't believe that should make a difference. What I do is more important than what I wear." He was a man of action. His part-time real estate career really excited him; his job was his security.

Cynthia was an agent for a large real estate company in the metropolitan area. An achiever, she had sold over a million dollars worth of property for three years in a row. Norman helped her, and together they succeeded in making money. But none of their great collaboration carried over into parenting.

Cynthia, tears trickling down her cheeks, sobbed, "He's just too hard on the children, especially Brad, *my* sixteen-year-old."

Whenever a parent claims a child as an individual accomplishment, flashing red lights go off in my mind. "Cynthia, did you hear yourself say 'my sixteen-year-old'?"

"Yes, I said that. Norman doesn't care about him. I'm his parent."

Norman and Cynthia had all the qualifications for successful, positive parenting. They were intellectually above average and socially refined. They were assertive and involved themselves in church life. They had a concern for physical fitness and earned enough money to do almost anything they chose. The problem was interpretation.

When do you decide you are a successful parent? When your son is sixteen? Hardly. "Train up a child in the way he should go: and when he is *old*, he will not depart from it." Sixteen is not old enough. Let's try forty. Here's my rule of parental perspective: Decide how good a parent you are when your child becomes forty.

Premature judgment rules out a lot of changes that time will make. At twenty, most of us are not just chronologically half of forty; we're *less* than half as mature as we'll be at forty. Why judge your parenting skills so early? How well you have modeled being a parent only shows up when your child becomes a parent himself and demonstrates what he has learned from you.

It is no accident that the cliché says, "Life begins at forty." By forty, enough sand has run through the hourglass to provide some insight. Perspective is the insight of years—plus experience—plus understanding. That trio of reality gives us a clear view of life.

Relax! Take some of the pressures off your life as a parent.

This is your book, as well as mine. I'll point the way through the parenting puzzle, but you must experience your own success or failure. Only you are an accurate judge.

Question: What can you do today to insure the success of your parenting forty years from now?

TWO

A Plan for Parenting

"It is your human environment that makes climate."
Mark Twain

Maxine was forty-seven years old. She cried softly, reaching for a tissue, struggling to tell her story. Her third child would graduate from college soon, and she finally faced a dreaded reality with which she had struggled for more than twenty years: depression. "I sensed, even when we dated, that Joe [her husband] came from a different world than I did, but I thought love would overcome. . . ."

Her voice trailed off in the choking emotion of more quiet sobs. She regained her control. "It wasn't as bad in the early years of our marriage. I tried so hard to be an understanding wife. I didn't intend to browbeat my husband. But when the children came along, I realized how far apart we were. I feel so alone now. My children have been my life. When Joe, Junior, gets married after graduation, I guess I'm through."

My mind is troubled by women like Maxine. I wonder if it could have been different for them. Can the same challenge—parenthood—be more satisfying for you?

Courtship reveals something about what parenting will

be like with your intended. His life's background shapes his ideas about personhood, both positively and negatively. We really have only two basic choices: We either want to be like our parents, in response to a healthy childhood, or we want to be unlike our parents, because of an unhappy childhood. What challenges us most is the necessity of being perceptive about our own lives. How do we decide which influences have shaped us the most?

Here are four "tests" of past influences to use in your thinking: the tests of association, attributes (basic characteristics), adjustment, and attitude. Gaining perpective on your own life is just as important as knowing your spouse.

Association

Memory courses often suggest that association improves recall. That's true in the emotional world, too. However, the associations often escape our conscious minds and therefore affect the way we react without providing an obvious, rational source for our behavior.

When couples have conflict, associations often express anger. "You're just like your mother," he says. That two-edged sword can destroy his wife. First, she resents his accusation. After all, she certainly knows her mother better than he does. She lived with her for nineteen years, and he can hardly stand her for nineteen days a year, when she arrives for her annual visit with her grandchildren. But even more damaging is the fact that she wants in so many ways *not* to be like her mother. A part of her hates her mother, and another part feels guilty for not loving her. Among the conflicting feelings she experiences at a time like this, a wife may remember her own vow to never be like her mother. Hearing her husband's accusation, she feels totally frustrated, defeated, and crushed. She bursts into tears. He feels guilty and comforts her, but the issues are never dealt with seriously.

I'm suggesting that you and your husband gather your courage and plan a time when both of you can ask questions about your childhood and the attitudes you developed along the way. This assignment cannot be described as easy, but the results are often extremely satisfying. Think these things through on your own, then discuss them with each other:

1. What are the ways I see myself like my mother? father?
2. Am I pleased with those associations, or do they concern me?
3. What do I see in my spouse that reminds me of his parents?
4. Does that reassure me or cause me uncertainty when I think of our parenting?
5. What can I tell my life partner about my fears in parenting?
6. Is there an association with my parents' behavior that I most want to avoid?
7. What change would I most like to see in the way he parents and what I know about the way his parents handled him?

Set aside at least an hour, preferably away from distractions like the telephone or television, and share with each other your feelings about these questions. As you prepare to share these things with your spouse, be honest in determining your relationship with your own parents. Learn the secret of living fearlessly by knowing yourself better than anyone else knows you.

Attributes

As you come to know yourself and evaluate your strengths for parenting, look at your partner's attributes, too. Is he an open, transparent person? Can you feel relaxed around him? Does he "wear well" in a relationship? Do you like him better, the more you get to know him? Does he respond only to direct questions, or does he generate discussions of feelings and ideas? Do you treat him with gentleness—the "kid-glove approach"—because of his temper or reactions?

The problems encountered in parenting exaggerate our past experiences. The quiet husband may well become the silent father. The husband inexperienced at showing affection will have difficulty touching and showing affection to his child. The harried wife will become the overburdened mother. Human beings continue in the same behavior pattern until they are either forced or taught to change it. Unfortunately, such changes too often result from pain, rather than pleasure. Conflicts, failures, frustrations, and negative encounters *force us* to change. On the other hand, positive reinforcement and learning *allow us* to change more creatively. Given the choice, most of us would prefer creative change. The parenting process should be entered into as carefully and positively as possible, and self-knowledge is an early step on that path.

Adjustment

How you handle stress may be a very specific key to your effectiveness as a parent. As you approach parenthood, you should gain some insight into your own mechanisms for stress control. Are you an escapist in the face of stress? Habits or drugs, such as alcohol or pills, may be indicators of this pattern. Withdrawal is another form of escape, as is denial through stoicism. So many people marry to leave home (another escape pattern), but don't deal with the pattern effectively until later in life. It is hard to escape from the responsibilities of parenting and lonely to cope with them unassisted. As you and your husband consider a child, it's essential you discuss your reactions to stress.

Attitude

Our life goals are shaped by our inner attitudes and hidden hopes. When you marry a man who has a case of wanderlust, he will without doubt either change or feel trapped and "held back" later in life. For him, fulfillment may lie in the amount of earth's territory explored, while you have the nesting instinct. Trouble looms on the horizon—not only for the marriage relationship, but in the raising of children. So many couples fail to confront these differences.

Lou appeared relaxed when he came into my office. He had the appearance of casual elegance. His shirt was silk and his slacks were fashionable. He professed satisfaction with his marriage to Ginger, but her obvious disappointment discouraged him. As we talked further, I discovered he held repressed feelings about freedom. The more room he needed to grow and develop, the more stringent Ginger's demands seemed to become.

When they had not been able to have children, he was ready to accept it and face the future as a childless couple. Ginger was adamant about adoption. Their selected son was healthy and beautiful, but very hyperactive. Soon Ginger's demands for relief from the burden of child care seemed to infringe on Lou's time for career development, and their marital quarrels increased.

"I think I could have coped with her needs, but having a child has pushed me over the edge," Lou said with bitter resignation. "I can't wait fifteen years for the freedom to live again." In the course of working through their immediate

21

crisis, Lou and Ginger learned the secret of successful parenting: marital intimacy.

The foundation of happiness as a parent is closeness to your spouse. It's obvious that your spouse will be around longer than your child, but the demands and pleasures of the child are immediate. The spouse's needs may take a secondary role because he is an adult, but his resentment at being displaced—a childlike fear and a childish response—may fester into an eruption in later years. The empty-nest syndrome tells more about the marriage relationship than about the parenting function. Without the presence of children, the relationship may no longer be fulfilling for one or both of the partners.

Preparenthood Planning

In addition to gaining self-knowledge and sharing the deepest feelings of your spouse, you can avoid parental problems by developing a "life plan for parenting." I'll detail this later, but outline it here. The plan has three basic ingredients—awareness, balance, and commitment: *awareness* of the couple's needs and desires (including parenting needs), *balance* in their approach to each other and the function of parenting, and *commitment*, first to the marriage, and then to the child. Nothing can be as good an insurance program against the empty-nest syndrome as this process.

THREE

Preparental Vows

> "The family you come from isn't as important as the family you're going to have."
> **Ring Lardner**

The church was filled with observers, and the wedding party had assembled at the front of the sanctuary. Almost everyone present had heard the words before, but they listened intently as the bride and groom repeated these words after the minister: "I take thee to be my faithful husband (wife). I pledge to be true in plenty and poverty, in joy and sorrow, in sickness and in health, as long as we both shall live." Those few words symbolically express the commitment a couple makes to each other in marriage. There are no words about children or parenting in the marriage vows, unless one interprets the "plenty" as being prechildren and the "poverty" as postchildren!

What expression would vows about children take? Let me suggest seven vows for the consideration of every couple expecting children, and perhaps as a guideline for review if you already have children.

Vow Number 1   I pledge never to forget that you have a name.

The most subtle change that takes place in parenting is that we shift our emphasis from a loving relationship to a shared function. How many couples do you know who call each other Mommy or Daddy, but rarely ever call each other by name? Worse yet is the substitution of those terms for the pet names or endearments we used to use.

Alice seemed confused about her marital vows. "Something is missing. We just don't seem to love each other the way we used to when we were first married," she said with an almost embarrassed look on her face. After talking with her about her children and some other developments across the fifteen years of their marriage, I began to change direction in the conversation, and called her by name.

She smiled for a moment, and I could tell by the look on her face that she was thinking of something else, so I stopped talking.

"I'm sorry," she said. "I just realized when you spoke my name that my husband hasn't used my name in so long that I can't remember. All he ever calls me is Mother. Don't misunderstand me. I love my children, but I like my name, too. I guess I feel more like a person than a role when I hear my name."

For the next few weeks, without being obvious, I listened to the couples I saw socially and professionally. Startlingly, few of them called each other by name. Some managed to nod in the other's direction at times. Occasionally a husband would say "my wife" when speaking to me. He would not only fail to speak his wife's name, but he usually didn't look at her when he talked to her. I needed no more convincing of the appropriateness of this pledge in the pre-parenting stage of life.

Call him Daddy if you like, but don't forget the Fred or Bill or Harry he was given at birth, or the nickname that he uses when he introduces himself to others and says, "My friends usually call me. . . ." Be a friend for life; call him by his name.

Vow Number 2   I pledge you priority in my life commitments.

While the 1980s are bringing some changes on the American scene as far as parental roles are concerned, an almost universal division of labor comes with parenting. Since women bear children, many men think women must care for the children. Even though these women may resent that unfortunate and unnecessary assumption, too many homemakers begin to think of themselves as mothers first and wives second. The resulting problems are felt by both husbands and wives.

Ralph slumped in his chair and ran on a good while with his monologue about how bad his life was. Almost thirty minutes of nonstop complaints had elapsed, when I finally got a question in quickly. "What would be the most important change your wife could make to improve your relationship?"

"Make me number one in her life," he shot back angrily. I asked how he got to be number two. As he talked about the birth of his children, he seemed resentful toward them. When I mentioned this to him, he said, "I'm not really resentful of my children. I'd just like to have my wife back to myself some of the time."

I'm sure that Ralph contributed to the problem with his self-pity, but their reputation in the community supported his feelings. They were both "superparents," presidents of the PTA at the school their children attended, workers in the refreshment booth at athletic events, and fund raisers for every cause involving children.

Dale was a very attractive woman, but she oozed jealousy in almost every comment she made about her husband. What had driven her into therapy was her own pain over her husband's affair with a younger woman. "How can I compete with her sexually or any other way? She's never even had a baby, and I've had two!"

"Tell me about your children," I interrupted.

At first she seemed puzzled, but eventually she was telling me about the "joys" of her life, the two preschoolers she had at home. "For the last five years, I've really concentrated on being a mother. . . ." Her voice trailed off as the impact of what she had said settled in her mind.

I was quick to point out that she could not take responsibility for her husband's relationship with another woman, but she could make some changes in the way she related to him. In a matter of a few weeks, both Dale and Ralph had recommitted themselves to each other in marriage, and Dale had made a rather interesting discovery. She described it this way: "I now know that I was jealous of the parenting role. I cherished my time with the children and used them as an excuse not to do with Ralph some of the things he wanted to share with me. I don't love my children any less now, but I think I've got my priorities in better order. I'm a wife first and a mother next."

Giving your marriage priority is a tough challenge. Two people must strive to give their relationship the best of their energy and opportunities for development. A successful marriage is more than work; it's a fine art, requiring discipline and "feel" in the relationship. The necessary sensitivity develops through stressing the priority of your commitment to each other.

Vow Number 3   I pledge to remember that it takes two to parent one.

Some parents find it difficult to say "our" children but easy to say "my" son or daughter. I recently ate alone in a restaurant while three couples occupied the table next to mine. I tried not to eavesdrop, but the volume of their voices and the proximity of the tables made it difficult not to be aware of them. One woman spoke emphatically about "my" child several times, until in the middle of a sentence, the man she was apparently married to said, "Hey, those are my kids, too. You didn't have them by yourself." They all laughed and went on with their conversation, but it reminded me of a poignant moment of reconciliation between a couple I had seen several days before in the office.

Jan was a bright girl, athletic and trim, and better than average in the appearance department. Harold was somewhat shy, a more ordinary type, and seemed to have difficulty winning points when they disagreed. Their marriage had conflicts in several areas, but one of the most significant seemed to be about the children.

She was just "smarter" as a parent than he. If he planned something with the children, she always seemed to have a better suggestion. If he corrected them, she told him later how he should have done it. Their relationship had deteriorated until a separation resulted. I frankly had little hope for them, until one afternoon in a joint appointment, she said, "Harold, I owe you an apology. I have been playing one-upmanship with you, especially with the children. I didn't realize it until yesterday, when Bobby was trying to build something. I told him to change what he was doing. He persisted until I intervened. He looked up and said, 'Mom, it may not be as good as you can do, but I want to do it my way.' His eyes flashed anger, but he later broke down and cried, telling me how much he missed you. I didn't sleep much last night, but I learned that it takes more to be a parent than just knowing the right way. I can't be a parent without you. Please come home." Harold was dropping tears on the lapel of his expensive suit by the time she finished her touching comments.

Jan said it better than I could; it takes two to parent one. That's true not only biologically but also emotionally and spiritually. While one parent may heroically succeed, in the face of the death of a spouse or an unwanted divorce, the natural order of things mandates that two parents have more to offer than one. Parenting is not a competition, but a cooperative effort between two bodies, minds, and souls. Take the pledge together!

Vow Number 4   I pledge to be polite when we disagree about parenting concepts.

An essential principle in the resolution of conflict is the ability to confront courteously. In my book *Try Marriage Before Divorce* (Word Books, 1978), I listed and discussed the six guidelines for managing conflict:

1. Handle it as it arises.
2. Confront courteously.
3. Stick to the issue.
4. Listen as much as you talk.
5. Listen to compromise.
6. Anticipate reconciliation.

Probably the most easily destroyed area of human interaction is the emotional climate. When a partner in marriage feels disregarded, his spirit is broken. He may become hostile. The atmosphere of marriage erodes, and the parenting partnership becomes undermined. No parent intends this result; it subtly occurs. Why?

Basically it results from the loss of a sense of politeness and courtesy in dealing with each other. Let me illustrate:

Paul was a successful businessman. He made money, and he looked the part, but I knew almost instantly that he was one of the angriest men I had ever met. You could almost see the smoke rising from his ears. "I can't stand being ignored around my own house." He fumed and fussed through a verbal upheaval that was the result of what he viewed as discourteous behavior. His wife and daughters may have been guilty. Preoccupied with things they felt only interested females, the women of the family had developed an attitude characterized by "the girls and Paul," a phrase repeated quite regularly in conversation. Paul's first reaction was feeling hurt at being left out, but he didn't express his feelings. Hurt is the other side of the coin of anger, and his pain eventually boiled over.

When the family finally met together in my office, their behavior became apparent to them. Susan, Paul's wife, felt no intentional animosity toward him, but she had drifted into a pattern of doing almost everything with the girls, with a minimum of consultation with Paul. She said it this way: "I wouldn't want to feel left out, either. I can see how that has happened. I really want us to be a foursome again."

Susan and Paul resolved their differences through a simple procedure. Each Sunday evening, they sat down with the girls and talked about the coming week's activities. Susan discovered that Paul was not only interested, but that he would volunteer to become involved in some of the girls' plans, relieving her of the chauffeuring responsibility. In a short time, the father-daughter relationships were much improved, and Susan and Paul found themselves planning more time together for couple activities. The restoration of the courtesy of discussing parental responsibilities played a significant role in improving their marital relationship.

Another incident comes to mind. Marian and Bob came from extremely different family backgrounds. His was "relaxed and laid back," as he described it. Hers was more formal and less affectionate. When their children came along, it was much easier for Bob to become the family entertainer. He spent a good deal of time playing with their babies. Both boys and their little girl enjoyed the camping trips, sporting events, and physical affection Bob showed.

Marian grew less affectionate toward him, refusing to respond sexually, and finally saying she wanted a divorce. By the time I saw them, the tension was high. "I have to carry all the disciplinary responsibility at our household. The kids call me an ogre because I have to make them do the difficult things, while Santa Claus only plays ball and treats them to outings. It isn't fair. I can't win in that kind of comparison," she summarized.

The word *win* gave me a clue that they felt competitive toward each other. Bob responded, "Is it wrong to enjoy your kids? They're good kids; they don't need that much correction. She's just so blooming perfectionistic—like her mother."

Before they got into a long tirade, I suggested a compromise plan. First, each of them was to write down the five most important things he or she expected the children to learn from him or her as a parent. When we got together again, we compared lists. Their goals were amazingly similar.

My job is to help people relate strengths more effectively. I believe most couples and families want to succeed in their relationships. What I did with Bob and Marian was to selectively ask what strengths in each of their backgrounds could help them accomplish these goals. It took only three or four sessions for them to begin to feel a mutual need for each other's strengths, rather than a competitive battle to be proven right about their philosophical differences in child-rearing. You've probably already guessed that this marriage improved dramatically.

This illustrates another basic tenet I have about family counseling: Happy marriages are the foundations for successful families. Good lovers, as a rule, make better parents. Why? Because they want to share with their children what they share with each other—a bond of closeness. A strained marriage infects the parent-child relationship with doubt, distance, and discouragement. It's hard to be a positive parent when you are a disenchanted spouse.

Keep your marriage alive by communicating as politely and pleasantly with each other as you do with your best friends. The dividends from this marital and parental pledge are inestimable. Treat your spouse as a perishable commodity, and you'll be surprised how long he lasts.

Vow Number 5   I pledge to be persuasive rather than demanding in our shared responsibilities as parents.

Driving through the rural sections of Georgia can be a tremendous learning experience. Some years ago I stopped on a country road and visited an old general store. It was the first time I remember seeing flypaper, a strip of brown paper with a sweet-smelling, sticky substance on it. The insects, attracted to the odor, stuck to the paper and died. I asked the proprietor of the store what the substance was. I don't remember his answer, but several men sitting around the store were amused by my ignorance. One of them spun off that bit of country wisdom, "You can catch more flies with honey than you can with vinegar." Persuasion works like honey.

Have you ever observed the subtle but real changes that seem to happen to the majority of couples as they live together, especially after they become parents? Early in the marriage, their eyes shine as they speak of each other, and they occasionally sneak half-embarrassed glances in the other's direction; they are obviously in love. Some years later, one of them can talk for ten minutes straight, while the other reads or watches television without really hearing the other's message. Later in the marriage, they may degenerate to saying things to each other through their children, rather than directly. When the children leave home, silence descends like a cloud of gloom. Extreme? No, all too *characteristic* of so many households. How could it be different? By following more closely the pledge of persuasion rather than demand.

Look at these three segments of conversation between parents at different stages in the lives of their children:

Example one: A two-year-old has been refused candy at 5:00 P.M. shortly before his father comes home from work. He cries and runs into his room. Dad arrives to find Mom tense and little Junior screaming in his room. "What's wrong?" he asks.

"I wouldn't let him have some candy, and he's been crying for ten minutes. Go in there and spank him for being such a spoiled brat," she responds.

If Dad greets his son with a spanking, he feels he has been manipulated into an unwanted conflict. If he doesn't, he is not giving her the support she requested.

Example two: Dad arrives home from work and begins blowing the car horn until Mother comes to remove the tricycles from the driveway. He emerges from the car, angrily shouting, "Haven't I told you to tell the kids to keep those tricycles in the garage?"

If she answers yes, she accepts the responsibility for enforcing his demands about the children's behavior. If she says no, he continues to be angry because his "laws" have been broken.

Example three: After turning off the lights, Jeff hears his wife crying. Turning over, he asks if she's all right. She explains how lonely she feels and how she was crushed earlier in the evening when he failed to support her in front of the children. "How can I accomplish anything with the kids if I don't have your support?" Jeff is frustrated because he doesn't feel guilty of nonsupport or think she has failed to accomplish anything with the children. He is also angry that she waited until midnight to confront him with this problem.

All three of these incidents can be handled with proper communication and understanding between the parents. Most people would expect that comment from a family counselor, but a recent meal with a judge of the superior court circuit yielded these comments when I asked what he had learned about parents from his years on the bench.

"I don't think they talk much," the judge said. "I'm not a psychologist, but I decided that most kids rebel against the law to try to find out if there are any limits in the world. They buffalo their parents and think they can ride roughshod over the rest of the world. I wish I truly believed prison would take the sneers off some of their faces. Too many of them just get hardened and become repeat offenders. It's a tragedy that the parents can't communicate with each other enough to teach their children some respect for the rights and privileges of others."

The judge was discouraged, but he was basically saying that parental vinegar isn't the best substance for your children. If your communication sours, it won't attract your children to the content of what you say. They will turn to others for the foundations of their philosophies about life. Teachers, other parents, television, and their peers will teach them what you won't.

To be persuasive rather than demanding requires a willingness to face disturbing and disagreeable situations with open options. Doing so with as much consideration as possible for each other and your children is the goal. Learning to understand what your spouse *means* when he says something builds the bridge of understanding, so he will listen when you try to explain your feelings. Such understanding leads to a mutual meeting—a compromise—which allows both partners to feel successful in working out solutions with each other. This climate of understanding and compromise will invite children to explore their own ideas without fear of judgment or rejection, and will give them an alternative to rebellion. You are winning the war when your children tell you negative things; that's an indication they trust you. Parents who can face honest differences and explore alternatives breed healthy assertiveness in each other and their children.

A crisis provides marital partners with an invitation to growth. Those who courageously accept these invitations will find new dimensions in their love relationships—first with each other and then with the children.

A crisis forces each of us to choose among various ways of reacting. One choice is a protective, manipulative style, where you telegraph the message that *your* wants and needs are paramount. On the other hand, a persuasive approach takes your feelings into account while considering the needs of your family members and the situation itself.

Committing yourself to the risky business of sharing opens new options for understanding and compromise. The partnership process is enhanced, and intimacy strengthened. The effort required by sharing is more than rewarded by the growth of the relationship.

Vow Number 6   I pledge to remember that parenting is as new to you as it is to me.

No matter how long it takes me to learn something, I often expect others to know it as soon as I tell them. So it is with parenting. My own parents may have spent years drilling an idea into my consciousness, and I probably doubted it each time they told me. However, when I discovered it worked, and shared the idea with my partner, she was expected to understand immediately, and to agree enthusiastically. *Wrong!*

To pledge yourself to be patient with your fellow parent sounds easy enough, but may be the most difficult of parental commitments. Just as the things that only aggravate us in our premarital experiences often infuriate us after we are married, the untapped differences we never dreamed existed before we became parents loom large on the living horizon.

Phil and Rebecca had a nine-month-old daughter. Both of them were twenty-four and wanted children early in their marriage. They were nearing their third anniversary when I saw them, but I got no impression of young love from their faces. Phil was rather stiff and rigid in demeanor. Rebecca looked strained and had those telltale water reservoirs around her eyes, just waiting for an excuse to rain tears. It didn't take long before they rolled down her cheeks, and Phil looked even more uncomfortable.

" 'Becca, please don't cry," he said, half-empathetically and half in frustration. I asked him what he thought her tears meant. "She's disappointed with being a mother" was his reply.

The tears stopped instantly as she retorted, "I am not. If anything, I think *you* aren't happy with being a father."

Their anger welled up for a few minutes, but eventually we pursued some of the meaning in back of the feelings they expressed toward each other. Rebecca assumed that since Phil didn't volunteer to do more things for the baby, he wasn't interested. When he told her how he felt, he admitted that he was frightened of hurting the child or doing the wrong thing. Before the session was over, Phil also admitted that he assumed Rebecca knew more about being a parent than he did, and he wanted her to tell him what she needed.

"I *have* told you what I need, but you ignore the opportunities," she replied. "Anyway, just because I bore Marcy doesn't make me any more intelligent about child rearing."

I suggested some ways they could try to ferret out their ideas and impressions about how parents should act. Phil was the oldest of two boys. As he talked about his experience of growing up, he shared the memory of his father, who was fifteen years older than his mother, sitting across the room from his younger brother's crib, smoking his pipe.

"What did he do for the baby?" I asked.

"I not only can't recall his touching my brother, I was seven, almost eight, and he rarely touched me, except a pat on the head now and then. I don't think he ever put his arms around me. I never remember him telling me that he loved me. 'Becca's family is so different—always hugging and kissing, and everybody says, 'I love you.'"

Rebecca remembered her physician father playing with both her young sisters and being very affectionate. She found Phil very affectionate to her, but thought it strange that he rarely held their daughter. As she began to understand her expectations for him as a father, she also shared more information with him about the baby. Phil found it easier to change his pattern and to make parenting more of a partnership in their home. He learned new behavior from Rebecca by adopting a role model quite different from his father.

This vignette can be an invitation for your present or potential parenting. Improve your chances of satisfaction by knowing as much as possible about each other's backgrounds and ideas about children. There are no right and wrong ways to parent; almost every home is different. The most effective way to be happy in early parenthood is to talk through your expectations of each other and find some common ideals to share. These questions may be helpful in uncovering your expectations:

1. *What is the earliest memory you have of being with your father or mother as a child?* What were you doing? How did you feel about your parent's part in that experience?_____

2. *What did your father almost always do with you as a young child?* Your mother? Did you wish for some particular activity with either of your parents? What have you said to yourself along the lines of, "When I have kids, I'll_____

3. *When you recall your parent of the opposite sex, in what ways do you hope your spouse will be like that parent?* In what ways do you hope your spouse is not like that parent?_____

The same kind of questions can be asked for later periods of development, but should be concentrated on the earliest childhood experiences in this initial phase of conversation.

Parenting is not automatic. Poor models for parenting only allow us to decide what we do not want to do. We must still develop positive patterns for our own experiences as parents. Patience may well be the supreme virtue in the parenting process, but direct it first to your spouse, then be patient with the children.

Vow Number 7　I pledge to give myself to the process of discovering my potential and yours as we parent together in life.

I liked Charlie Shedd's title *You Can Be a Great Parent.* Like so much of what he writes, it invites us to be *better* than we have been. The beauty of a concept of potential in parenting is that we don't ever have to stagnate. Potential is my way of dreaming in life. Robert Browning once said that a man's reach should always exceed his grasp. Potential is for the reachers!

Too often, parenting gets hung up on the priority level. Because children can be—and usually are—demanding, we tend to meet the moment and deal with it. There are some things that *have* to be done for, with, and about children. Parents gladly give their children that kind of time. From the emotional crises that don't seem to be on any schedule to the physical crises that never arrive at a convenient time, we face a level of insistence in our children's lives. But we will fail miserably if we always function at that level in our parenting. A progressive step up comes when parent and child can begin to do some preplanning for facing the emergencies and events that are certain to come.

Parents need to protect themselves and their time by looking ahead and thinking through situations children may face. It's *priority parenting* when I rescue my child from the curb as a stranger offers him a ride. It's *progressive parenting* when I describe those situations and let my child think through his options for behavior *before* the incident arises. I reach my potential as a parent when my child begins to ask me about situations and how I would handle them. I'm his consultant at that point, and that's the position I'm going to occupy when he finally reaches his independent state of adulthood.

If that's the goal with my children (and it is), why not have the same kind of positive progression with my partner in parenting? Jim and Betty were caught up in a thorny conflict when I first consulted them. They sincerely tried to be Christian parents. They read the Bible together, attended conferences, and listened to what some of the speakers and advisors suggested. But it didn't seem to work.

They seemed to have particular difficulty with the "umbrella" theory of accountability they had learned. They were trying to practice God first, husband next, wife third, and children last in line in this basic system, but they became increasingly frustrated in practice. Betty confided in me, "I love Jim and respect him, but I resent being a second lieutenant, almost reporting to him for decisions and authority. I have to use my own brain and do some things I can be responsible for myself, otherwise I begin to feel unnecessary."

Jim was almost afraid to question this concept that he thought was biblical. "I want to do what's right, Doctor, but I really feel Betty is at least as capable as I am in parenting. I try to be the head of the family and fulfill my God-given role as a father, but I find it hard to deal with some of the discipline questions when I come home."

I offered Jim and Betty an alternative plan for parenting—the consultant pattern. In business, when a proprietor needs help, he may hire a consultant with whom he shares the problem and from whom he gains support and advice which may not be available from his employees or within the company. It is the responsibility of the owner or chief executive officer of any corporation to seek consultation when he needs it. God has so arranged the parenting process that we get a built-in consultant. Being a parent alone is a staggering responsibility—ask any widow or parent who bears the brunt of the burden by himself.

The marriage partnership provides the ideal inner sharing opportunity. Within a trusting, confidential relationship, I can not only safely bare my own fears, but can receive input from someone who cherishes me as a person and shares the responsibility for the children. That kind of consultation is priceless. That's the ideal for the family—a marriage partnership in which each parent supports and consults with the other parent in the various responsibilities of child rearing.

Obviously, the ideal is not real in a lot of homes. Two patterns of failure emerge from my counseling files: One is competitive in nature, and the other is the "carbon copy," or isolationist, pattern.

The competitive parent   Competition ranks in a tie with any other destructive force in a marriage relationship. When this attitude infects the parenting process, the contest is staged in the lives of the children. Confusion results. Parents who try to outdo each other place their children in untenable positions, since the child feels he must either approve or disapprove of his parents' efforts. Ultimately this makes the child the emotional nurturer, or parent, in the home. Much like the situation that exists when parents divorce, the child feels torn; he loves both parents, but often feels he must be loyal to the weaker (or wronged) parent.

Nancy's mother had been an alcoholic during most of her maturing years at home. Even though her mother now attended Alcoholics Anonymous and had been sober for several years, Nancy found herself constrained to call her mother regularly to check on how she was. This pressure was reflected when Nancy and her husband came for counseling because their own daughter was doing so poorly in school. In our sessions, Nancy not only identified the feeling that she had been her mother's emotional parent since her childhood, but she recognized how much her parents had competed for her attention and approval.

"Mother would feel guilty about drinking and take me shopping when she sobered up. Daddy took me out to eat and to the movies when she was drinking. Even when I was young, I felt like we were all avoiding the problem. I can remember both of them saying to me, 'Don't think badly of me, Nancy. I'm doing the best I can in this marriage.'" The bottom line was that Nancy felt torn. She nurtured both parents through the years when she needed that essential nurturing herself, in order to develop her own capacity.

Unfortunately, it not only affected her choice of a marriage partner, but contributed to the same pattern in her marital relationship. When I asked her how she was competing for her own daughter's attention, Nancy seemed stunned. Later she could see that by withdrawing, she forced her daughter to attempt to get her attention. The child's disciplinary and study problems began to change almost overnight when Nancy made some direct attempts to nurture her daughter. Her parents' competition had sabotaged her own ability to see what she was doing as a parent.

Competitiveness can be seen in Nancy's example, but it takes many other forms, such as attempting to outdo each other in activities, playing Santa Claus year-round with gifts, or being overly permissive and thereby leaving the disciplinary role to the other parent.

The "carbon-copy" parent. The other major pattern in parental failure is the "carbon copy," or isolationist, approach. Men are very susceptible to this problem, particularly when they override their wives' disciplinary action. The wife becomes a "carbon copy"—only free to repeat what has been said or done in the home, but not adding or changing anything.

Ralph grew up in a home where his father's word was law. His own somewhat macho style made that an easy model for him to adopt in parenting. Michelle, his intelligent but very intimidated wife, had been hospitalized three times for nervous breakdowns since their children had been born. "I can't depend on her for anything," Ralph fumed. "I've told her and the kids what the rules are, but she won't even enforce them when I'm not at home." As I gently tried to draw Michelle into the conversation, Ralph continued to dominate and interrupt. I finally got his attention when I mentioned his *three* children. "I only have two, Doc," he said.

I responded, "Well, I was including Michelle."

"I sometimes feel like I have three," he said.

Michelle's retort was, "He treats me like a child. Why shouldn't I behave like one?" The core issue had been identified in their parenting problems: Ralph was the only parent in the family! All he wanted from Michelle (at least it appeared this way) was having his decisions carried out. He finally admitted that he was lonely. Eventually they made attempts to become partners in the parenting process.

Either parent can be the isolationist. You can dominate and thereby rule your partner in the parenting process, or you can withdraw and leave all the responsibility to your spouse. Neither solution is satisfactory. The secret of successful parenting comes through the consultative model, where both parents respect each other, need each other, and have capabilities to contribute to the process. Neither parent can succeed alone as well as the two can succeed together.

The pledge of potential is a pattern of lifelong respect for each other, reflecting the opportunity to consult and share as each parent fulfills his or her total potential (capability).

These are the seven preparenting vows:

The Vow of Personhood	I pledge never to forget that you have a name.
The Vow of Priority	I pledge you priority in my life commitments.
The Vow of Partnership	I pledge to remember that it takes two to parent one.
The Vow of Politeness	I pledge to be polite when we disagree about parenting concepts.
The Vow of Persuasion	I pledge to be persuasive rather than demanding in our shared responsibilities as parents.
The Vow of Patience	I pledge to remember that parenting is as new to you as it is to me.
The Vow of Potential	I pledge to give myself to the process of discovering my potential and yours as we parent together in life.

These are my suggested promises for parents. If you are planning children, these ideas may spark some personal pledges you'll want to write down before the birth of your offspring. If you are already parents, these may suggest some other pledges you will want to share with each other. They may provoke some discussions about similarities between the experiences noted and your own. Parenting is such an unlimited opportunity, let this chapter be like eating that first potato chip.

FOUR

Preparation
for Parenting

"To heir is human."
Dolores McGuire

When I wrote *Being a Man in a Woman's World,* I thought back on my boyhood days in the Clearwater, Florida, area. Several major league baseball teams held spring training camps there. Babe Ruth was the home-run king of baseball. Although he had retired, he sat in the stands almost every day and watched the exhibition games. Spring training gives the manager a chance to evaluate the potential that rookie players have for making the roster of the big-league club. The new recruits get lots of scrutiny and instruction, both from the coaches and from teammates. It's such a natural way to learn the guidelines of your team.

Parenting does not have a spring training camp! Each couple gets some instruction from a physician or friends about what to expect in pregnancy, and perhaps the mother-to-be gets gifts from female friends at a shower, but that's about it. In the past (and in other cultures), the extended family not only helped instruct the prospective parents, but also assisted in the early years of the child. Whatever values there are in today's monogamous, nuclear

45

family, the extended family network once offered some valuable positive supports and approaches. Today, many young, prospective parents are not near their parents, grandparents or other family members. This chapter includes a suggestion for doing your own research and development to learn about parenting.

The ultimate responsibility for your parenting success belongs to you, not to your parents for what they did or did not do for you. Being creative rather than limiting will open doors for learning and gaining your goal: to be the best possible person in parenting that you can.

Developing Perspective

The first stage of any successful venture is developing perspective—seeing clearly what the expectations and problems may be in a situation. Parenting is no different. If the two of you came from very similar backgrounds in which you were supremely happy, these suggestions may not be useful. But, if you have some questions or ideas you'd like to explore about parenting, these proposals may prove not only stimulating, but exciting.

Pick the brains of the experts. Many successful people follow this principle: Where you don't have expertise, borrow it or buy it. There's an anecdote from the life of Henry Ford that illustrates this point of view beautifully. It seems that Mr. Ford was in court and was being cross-examined by an attorney as to his understanding of certain very complicated parts of the auto-making industry. Mr. Ford is said to have responded, "I don't understand all you are asking me, but if you'll give me fifteen minutes, I have someone here who can answer all your questions." That's management. What you don't know yourself, you learn from others.

The principle works in the parenting process, too. Since you can't *buy* skills in parenting, borrow them from those people you know who impress you as being the most successful at parenting. To get a variety of ideas, don't pick just young parents with small children. Find about twelve couples—three who have small children, three who have grade-school-age children, three who have high-school or college-age children, and three whose children are grown. If the two of you are very social, invite them all over for a "prepare us for parenthood" evening. Tell them in advance you'd like to discuss the joys *and* problems of being parents. No one can resist talking about himself or his children, even if he's not really an expert. Begin your discussion with the positives. Have some starter comments or questions prepared, such as, "My spouse and I want to be the best parents we can be. What secrets would you share with us from your experience as parents? What is your greatest satisfaction as a parent? How did the two of you develop your partnership in parenting?"

After each of the couples has shared along those lines, dig a little deeper (but gently) with queries like: "Can you share with us any problems that have been most difficult for you as parents? What is the biggest pitfall or disappointment you have had as a parent? What would you do differently if you could do it over with your children?" Depending on how well you know these friends and how well they know one another, this may prove to be one of the most enlightening evenings of their lives. Your questions can be very helpful in evaluating parenting, both for you and your friends.

If you're not comfortable with gathering a group together, the same basic idea can be used with one or two couples at a time. What has happened for the couples who have experienced this process is a sense of bonding together. These friends may become surrogate grandparents, aunts and uncles, or just closer friends who are not only concerned for you as a couple, but for your children. Several couples have chosen godparents for their children from these experiences. Others have gained caring friends as volunteer baby-sitters, or have been exposed to the children of these friends, thereby becoming more comfortable with the idea of having a baby or child around the home.

Resistant?

Maybe you're reading this and thinking, "I could never do that!" Let me tell you about Ken and Christine. Ken had to be one of the nicest guys I've ever met, but he was painfully shy. Christine, as you might expect, was the more outgoing type. When they met, her maternal instincts were fired high by this obviously sensitive and kind child-man. But she discovered great strength in him, and they had developed a good relationship. Their obstetrician had referred them to me for help with some sexual difficulties while she assisted them in becoming pregnant.

Christine had finally gotten pregnant, and they were nearing the six-month mark when they invited three couples from their congregation over for dessert and their attempt at learning from other parents. The evening became so stimulating for the four couples that one of the others offered to be hosts for a second meeting. Without planning it, these four couples became a sharing group and have become the best of friends through Ken and Christine's initial invitation. That may not happen from your experiment, but your willingness to learn from others is bound to have some interesting and positive effects, not only on the two of you, but also on those with whom you share.

A couple of grandparents came to me after a similar session to say how pleased they were to have been invited to share with the younger couples. Their own children lived at a distance, and even the visits they had with their grandchildren seemed too infrequent. "It made us feel good to think we could contribute something to these kids," Mack said. "And I told Maggie I had some new ideas about how to treat our kids because of what they said to us. You know, Doc, if this catches on, folks around here will have some real nice evenings together." An invitation to talk about what you've learned as a parent is a great compliment. I believe the most significant gift we can give another individual is the gift of attention. I have discovered I can learn something from almost anyone, if I listen to him.

Don't be afraid to experiment with an idea like this as you prepare for parenthood. If you are willing to admit that you are struggling with a particular problem, learning what other friends have done to overcome that difficulty may be a priceless asset.

I'd also suggest that any couple expecting a child learn to talk to God and ask for help in the parenting process. Cultivating your spiritual resources is a natural step toward preparing for survival in the parenting challenge.

FIVE

Learning to Pray About Parenting

"Pray without ceasing."
1 Thessalonians 5:17

My Roman Catholic friends pray for the dead. Patriots of all countries honor their dead. I was fascinated by the Chinese custom of grave sweeping, or cleaning, which comes annually in the spring, when the graves of ancestors are decorated and spruced up on a type of national holiday. We remember those who have lived before us and sometimes with us. Let's give more thought to preparation for those who will live with us and after us.

The Bible has numerous stories about people who prayed to be blessed with children. One of the most interesting tells of a woman named Hannah, whose husband, Elkanah, loved her very deeply (*see* 1 Samuel). That love alone could not relieve the pain she experienced in being childless. It became a spiritual exercise for her and required prayer and counseling with her priest, who joined in her request before God. Finally Hannah conceived and had a son who was named Samuel. She presented him as a young child to God, and he lived in the temple, learning the priesthood. Hannah had five other children after Samuel.

For some people, having children happens so easily. Other men and women seem to struggle to achieve pregnancy. One of the most excellent self-help groups for childless couples is called RESOLVE. Apparently there was no group like this available for Hannah, but she suffered through the ordeal of childlessness with only the support of her husband. He apparently loved her devotedly, but the grief was still difficult to bear. Some of the more sensitive gynecologists I know have referred couples to me during their struggle for pregnancy. It is an extremely difficult time, for both husbands and wives. The feeling of failing because you cannot produce a pregnancy is devastating. Once pleasurable sexual activity becomes routine because of the demand nature of the regimen prescribed for maximizing the opportunity for conception. Depression affects sexual performance. Deep understanding is needed by both partners during this time. The more private your nature, the more difficult these circumstances may become. If the two of you are there, maybe Hannah and Elkanah's experience can offer some guidelines.

I don't believe that a barren womb is a punishment from God, but Hannah felt that. For her, pregnancy became not only a cultural issue but a spiritual one. She felt despised by women who had given birth. Hannah became preoccupied with her problem. She didn't realize that there were days when her Israelite sisters would have gladly given her one of their children, just for a little relief! Her preoccupation did something positive for her, though; it provided the stimulus for an increasingly meaningful prayer life.

Parenting can do the same for us. If you don't learn to pray before your children are born, they'll teach you to pray when they become teenagers! The opportunity of sharing in the divine process of creativity can be a deepening experience for any one of us. Here are some thoughts and prayers for yourselves and your unborn child.

A Prayer for Appreciation of the Creative Process

Lord, forgive us for the things we so easily take for granted. We have taken for granted the matchless privilege of producing life. Give us a fresh appreciation that You share with us the mystery of creation and the amazing process of growth that occurs from our sexuality. Teach us both to cherish the possibility of creating a life into which You will breathe the essence of humanity.

Like Hannah and Elkanah, let us expect a child from You and be willing to dedicate that child as living proof not only of our love for each other, but also of our trust in Your answers to our prayers. Grant us the wonder of faith as we unite in love. May Your name be honored in our marriage and our parenting. *Amen.*

Rick and Karen had been married ten years when I met them. They now had three children, almost systematically planned, aged six, four, and two.

Karen loved children—all children—but especially her own. She had spent time before her own pregnancy working as a pediatric nurse. She continued to work a weekend shift in that ward. "We call it the Kid's Suite of the hospital."

Rick had been pretty quiet during the opening moments of our meeting. "I guess you'd like us to get to the point, huh, Doc?"

I nodded, but Karen interrupted. "It's my idea for us to be here. He has to change, or we'll see a divorce lawyer."

"What does he need to change?" I asked.

"He never helps with the kids. I have to get a baby-sitter, even when I work weekends."

Rick attempted to defend his work schedule as a high-school athletic coach. "A lot of our practices and games are on the weekends."

I sensed they had not yet gotten to the real issue when Karen burst into tears as she said, "He has plenty of time to pursue another woman."

The story sounded familiar, but with a twist. Karen really was good with her children and wanted to do everything for them. Rick failed to assert himself in his role as father, and soon felt left out. Though he somehow knew he had some responsibilities, he began to feel neglected, both as father and husband. He spent more time away from home and took a second job "because we could use the money." That added to the problem. Now he felt left out, and he was actually away and feeling sorry for himself.

In his new job an attractive woman began to pay attention to him and to share some of her own needs as they developed a friendship. It was a situation ripe for an affair, but Karen called one day for Rick and the woman answered the phone. In their conversation, Karen identified herself as Rick's wife. Fortunately the relationship cooled before they became more deeply involved. Karen later found a note in one of Rick's uniforms from the same woman, and Rick confessed his "little games," which he continued to say were all innocent fun. That brought them to my office.

Karen was now bitter that she had been working hard at being homemaker, mother, and part-time nurse while Rick had been playing. As the conversation developed, Rick finally exploded, "What about me? Am I just a machine to get you pregnant and pay bills so that you can have a family with *your* kids?"

Obviously the ideal in having children is a shared development of intimacy, but too many experience something less than that. Instead of increasing the level of shared commitment, a somewhat competitive element may develop. A time of great risk comes in the marriage. Many women find a newfound sense of fulfillment in the birth of a child; many men feel frustrated. One young husband said, "The only thing I can tell you is that I feel the way I did at the wedding rehearsal. I was there so that she and her mother could get on with their show." The presumed sharing does not develop as anticipated. Here's a prayer for the building of continued intimacy.

A Prayer for an Unbreakable Bond of Intimacy

We thank You, God, for the experience of loving each other deeply. Teach us to cherish our relationship, so we will not take each other for granted. Protect us from the erosion of tenderness that has robbed others of the joy of living with each other. Keep us thankful for being together, and deliver us from the temptation to give up emotionally when things become difficult. Teach us to grow toward each other and with You in the beauty of intimacy.

May our bond of love be so unbreakable that we may walk hand in hand with each other and under the shelter of Your arms until one shall lay the other at Your feet. Help us to experience fully this love, and allow us to teach our children how to love You and know the meaning of marital commitment. In Jesus' name. *Amen.*

Surrender is not a word that most of us enjoy. It is too often associated with defeat in a negative sense. In love, it is a paradoxical word: I give up, but I discover that I gain in the process. Jesus taught three paradoxes: lose to gain, give to get, and die to live. Those are the unalterable oddities of family living, too.

55

As the monarch cries in *The King and I*, "'Tis a puzzlement!" We, too, scratch our heads during the learning processes of life. It seems absurd that the more vulnerable we are to each other, the stronger our commitment grows. As we honestly know each other's weaknesses, we may develop a greater sense of protective radar within the relationship.

A friend of mine has written a book called *Courage for Crisis Living*. It is not about the parenting process, but the title summarizes what the bond of intimacy creates in a marriage relationship. *Intimacy* is an elusive word in our language. My definition is that intimacy is the soil from which both spirituality and sensuality grow. With intimacy, risk taking and trust produce the courage to face whatever challenges come our way. So, the intimacy that frees us to courageous living in the family develops from our physical and spiritual trusting of each other with the depths of ur beings.

A Prayer for Surrender of Ourselves and Our Child

O God, Your loving hand touches life in so many ways. We ask together for the gift of a child to bless and enhance our love for each other and for Thee. We know that all life is a gift from You, and we commit this unborn baby by our faith as a symbol of our dedication to Your will for us. Teach us to expect the bounty of Your blessings in gratitude and to give the best of our living in appreciation.

We cherish the guidance that brought us to each other as Your will, as we anticipate with joy the fulfillment of our love and the wonder of Your blessed creation, through us, of another life on earth. We surrender all that we are now and all we shall be together in thanksgiving for Your undeserved love. *Amen.*

A Prayer for Unselfishness

Lord, stretch the limits of our loving, that we may learn Your unselfishness. Teach us how to lay down our lives for each other, for our children, and for those to whom we are given, as You laid down Your own life for us. Save us from a limited view of the world, and grant us to see all people through Your eyes.

Help us to encourage each other in growth by reaching for our best goals and highest visions, rather than settling for easy victories and attainable marks. May these efforts be directed toward the good of others as well as our own benefit. Direct our lives so that our marriage, our family living, our career aspirations, and our wider involvements will bring glory to Your name. For Jesus' sake. *Amen.*

Perhaps nothing has forced me to learn to pray quite as much as the experiences I've had with children. When my oldest was just an infant and I was a twenty-three-year-old pastor in southern California, the phone interrupted the quietness of the night, and I was called to the hospital to be with another young family whose child, born a few minutes before, was not expected to live. By the time I arrived at the hospital, the baby's struggle had ended. The mother had been sedated, and the father and I stood with the doctor, who felt as helpless as I did. I prayed briefly with the two men, and when the doctor left, the young father put his arms around me and broke into sobs. I learned then that the hardest thing to do with our children is to give them up to death, but I also began to conceptualize a living axiom for myself: It is even harder to give our children up to life. That means to surrender them symbolically to God and His plan for their lives, but even more, to allow them the freedom to live free of our expectations and limitations. Praying every day for your child is one way to remind yourself that only God and that child can determine what is best for him in life. I have learned that it is also a wonderful way to discover strength in the daily process of parenting. We are not alone; even in the toughest times, God is there with us and our children.

A Prayer for Wisdom

O God, how marvelously You have made life. Forgive us for wanting too little knowledge of Your world, and teach us the wisdom of believing You in every area of living. Grant us to be whole in humanity, honest, open, and growing. Give us wisdom to be parents who not only want the best for our children but teach them to believe in Your love, which makes all things work for good to them.

Make us transparent windows of Your encouragement to others. Help us experience the victory of surrendering to You our will and the satisfaction of sacrifice in our daily living. Fill the empty spaces in Your world through us, that we may have the joy of being partners in Your creative process. Love Your children through us, and love us through them. In the name of Your Son, Jesus. *Amen.*

A Prayer for Patience in Parenting

O God, we thank You for Your eternal patience with us, Your children. Teach us to show the same tenderness to those lives You have given into our family. Give us perceptive eyes to see their struggles correctly. Sensitize our spirits to the inner pattern You have placed in each of them. Keep our short-fused judgment in check, except where our quickness will protect them from danger. Lead us and our children in the right paths, even if they are sometimes difficult.

Give us an unflinching faith in You and the ability to transmit the joy of that to our children by confidence in them. May our parenting be so according to Your plan that they will find it natural to call You Father. To the glory of Your Son. *Amen.*

A Prayer for Giving-up Grace

Lord, You entrusted these children to us so that we could experience more of Your love. They have been so beautiful in growing up that we fear letting them go. Not that we don't trust them to Your care, but the empty spots created when they leave home are like bottomless pits to fill. Only Your love can fulfill our needs. Teach us how to let our children grow up and gain independence, so that we can be friends when they no longer need to lean on us.

Keep us from loving them less because it will hurt to lose them. Somehow may we learn the meaning of losing in order to save. Teach us that the love we give away is really the only love we keep. Thank You for the grace to give them up to You now and to life later.

Help us to cherish them when they are our responsibility and to enjoy them when their friendship is our privilege. To Your glory. *Amen.*

PART TWO

Parenting
Priorities

"Ah! what would the world be to us
If the children were no more?
We should dread the desert behind us
Worse than the dark before."
Henry Wadsworth Longfellow

SIX

Love Your Child Responsibly

"Children in a family are like flowers in a bouquet: there's always one determined to face in an opposite direction from the way the arranger desires."

Marcelene Cox

Joan was a mature woman, almost forty-five, but she sobbed like a little girl whose heart had been broken. "I feel like such a failure. I don't think my children love me. I don't know what to do with myself." She mumbled through her linen handkerchief, between dabbing at the mascara running from her eyelashes. The fear she expressed characterizes too many parents: What if my children don't love me?

This is the heart of the matter: To be a parent is not to compete for the love or approval of your child. The parental responsibility is to love. You are not responsible for how your children respond to your love!

Parents step into quicksand when they begin to play the "I want you to love me" game with their children. I would be insensitive if I didn't acknowledge that almost all parents would like their children to love them *as* they grow up and *after* they grow up. Too often we try so hard while they grow up that they demand space from us after they've reached a point of chronological maturity.

Josh, at twenty-two, had gained some maturity. He said, in talking about his parents, "I assume they love me now and loved me then, but they failed to show me while I was growing up. They tried to buy me with gifts and make me happy by doing whatever I wanted to do. That's okay, I guess. In some ways it was really nice of them, but I often thought they were afraid of offending me more than they loved me." Josh had lovely parents. I knew them. They were pillars of the community, such nice people. They rarely had a conflict with anyone. That style had carried over into their parenting; they avoided discord by agreeing with the people around them, including their children. The result was a permissive parenting style.

Permissive Parenting

Two elements are constantly at work in child rearing: support and control. The permissive parent offers high support and little control. While the child may be told he is loved, he probably feels insecure. The result is usually the opposite of what the parents expect. The child rebels or seeks reassurance that he is taken seriously in other relationships. He feels his parents approve of him, but he lacks the structure for dealing with the rest of the world. His behavior may then be devious. He's looking for limits or discovering what he has to do for disapproval.

To love a child does not mean constant approval and support. Parental responsibility centers around helping the child build the boundaries of reality in such a way that not only are his personal feelings well developed, but that he can deal with the world outside himself. The permissive parent fails to take himself seriously enough in the process of modeling. The child instinctively begins to realize that something is wrong and seeks ways to right the circumstances in his life.

Priscilla was a pretty girl. She was "fifteen going on thirty-five." The tight jeans, the high-heeled shoes, and the symbol T-shirt all fit the image. Her makeup seemed overdone. She gave the external picture of sophistication. She maintained this image through two sessions. In the third hour, she finally blurted out, "I get away with murder! If my parents cared about me, they would rein me in. But they don't care." How tragic, but true, her analysis! Her parents were lovely middle-class southern people who had moved to Atlanta from a smaller metropolis and who wanted their daughter to be accepted by "society." They gave their daughter plenty of support, but almost no control. That's where they failed to love.

True love is demanding, not just devoted. Parents who want their children to mature fully will be willing to love them enough to set limits, provide structure, and teach values, but not just for the children's sake; parents need to do these things for themselves. A committed parent won't turn over his responsibility to the school or church or government; he wants to share his values with his children. The permissive style robs him of that opportunity.

Permissiveness does not fail because of the absence of quality time with the children. They will feel they have their parents behind them, but they won't have the safety of knowing what's expected of them. Like ships sailing into a dark harbor, children look for clear lights to follow. Otherwise, they crash on the rocks they cannot see and avoid.

Negligent Parenting

This parenting style offers neither enough support nor control. Where the permissive parent fails to control, the negligent parent fails both to structure and to support. From a practical standpoint, he is an absentee parent. His body is there, but he offers little of himself.

Gary was sent to me by the juvenile justice system through an arrangement made by his attorney. He was the father of a delinquent boy. Perhaps in reality there are no delinquent children, only delinquent parents; just as there are really no illegitimate children, only unmarried (or illegitimate) parents. Gary's youngish face hid some of the agony behind it. He worked two jobs, and he had come to my office dressed for his night job as a mechanic for a truck company.

"I wouldn't be here if it weren't for that kid of mine, Doc. I'm going to be late for work as it is," were his opening lines. In the course of the thirty minute monologue that followed, he justified his lack of parenting through financial pressure, his wife's "falling down on the job," and his disobedient son. When I asked him to describe his son's disobedience, he said, "I just want him to be a good kid and keep out of the way—not get in trouble—that's all."

I began to understand why his son had run away from home at age nine. Gary was the typical negligent parent. No, he was not a bad man. In fact, he was a hard worker, provided well for his family in the material realm, and didn't make any personal demands on his wife or children. As his wife put it, "The kids know he comes home to sleep. They have to be quiet in the mornings before they go to school. We have money; we just don't have a daddy." The whole problem was not of Gary's making, but negligent parenting has devastating results.

Little Tommy, who had run away, said, "They wouldn't miss me. All I ever hear is, 'Go buy yourself an ice cream. Go out and play. Go to your room.' I saw this movie on TV about a boy who ran away and got put in an orphanage. Maybe they'll send me there." What Tommy so amazingly expressed was that he wanted to be loved by his parents. If they couldn't or wouldn't, he was going to look for love somewhere else.

Looking for Love in the Right Place

The other day a popular song was playing on my car radio. One line reminded me that we don't always look for love in the best places. Less than twenty-four hours before, I had seen a rather disturbed young woman who sought love from her family but felt terribly rejected. It caused me to ask, where *should* we look for love?

The first place most of us turn is to our families. Most of us discover more latitude for our little quirks and failures in our homes than from any other source. But what if we look there and find no love or acceptance? An emptiness occurs in our lives.

To fill that gap many turn to therapy, looking for a missing ingredient in their lives. When they discover it, there is growth and development. If they do not, they may experience a sense of emotional handicapping, hindering much of their living.

Today is a good time to ask how we make sure our children and other members of our families find what they need when they turn homeward. Here are some suggestions to develop in your family:

1. *Make home a place where each member of the family can be sure of being heard.* No matter how unusual the idea may be, listen and try to understand. Assume that what your family mem-

ber says makes sense to him, even when you don't fully understand.

2. *Develop a sense of supportiveness with your honesty.* Stick together by assuming the positive about each other, even when a problem is faced. Let nothing divide you; no problem is too big for a family to face and share together. If it can't be handled within the family, seek professional advice from your physician, minister or therapist.

3. *Reinforce the bond of acceptance by expressing gratitude to your family members for their support.* A parent is at his best when modeling appreciation.

A child will find love when he looks for it in this kind of home.

Negligent parents tend to contribute rebellious, unruly, and runaway children to the society in which they live. They fail to create rules for their children, and tend to convey an attitude that the children are a difficult responsibility.

Authoritarian Parenting

Another familiar parenting style is the all-control–low-support motif. The "General Pattons" of the parenting world emerge here. They believe the old adage, "Children are to be seen and not heard." The motto of the parent of this type is: Children exist to be ruled by their parents. In fact, they really believe their children cannot get along without them. Their decisions cover every situation. Usually the family has a rule to fit the circumstance. Children grow up feeling wrong a good deal of the time. They hear a steady diet of *ought, should, must, don't,* and so forth. These parents don't understand Lord Chesterfield's cryptic comment, "Children and subjects are much seldomer in the wrong than parents and kings."

Clarise was twenty-one, with a somewhat childlike appearance, but smartly dressed in her airline flight-attendant clothing when she came to my office. "I have to fly in two hours after I leave, or I wouldn't have worn my uniform," she apologized. "My daddy wants you to send the bills for my therapy to him," she continued.

That seemed like a good place to start with her, so I asked about her money management. What I discovered was that she had not really left home, although she lived in an apartment near the airport with another flight attendant. Her checks were deposited in a bank 400 miles away, and her father covered any overdrafts that occurred in her account, as he had done since she was in college. The picture was becoming clearer. My task was to help this twenty-one-year-old child leave home emotionally. It took several months of gently reassuring her she could make decisions on her own, and several angry phone calls from her father. He referred to his daughter regularly as "my little girl."

I'm sure this gentleman loved his daughter and thought he was being the best parent he could be, but he had robbed his daughter of confidence and the opportunity of growing up to be independent.

Authoritarian parents often produce highly dependent but sometimes resentful children. Even when they leave home, they often feel the pressure of parental second-guessing and judgment when they make errors in the management of their lives. Often these children wind up returning home and living with their parents.

Combination of Styles

Before turning to the positive parenting style, I must mention that most couples differ in their ideas about their children. This makes being parented even more confusing for their children. For example, an authoritarian father may be married to a permissive mother. They reinforce each other's position. Dad becomes more demanding because Mom is too easy. Mom compensates for Dad's toughness by being more supportive. Dad makes his boy earn money, while Mom slips him a little extra because she loves him!

Another easily recognized pattern is the reverse—the authoritarian mother and the permissive father. Do you remember Fibber McGee and Molly or Dagwood and Blondie? Dad compensates for Mom's dominance by being a "pal" to the kids. She winds up handling most of the discipline and the major responsibilities.

You can probably identify many of the influences in your early life by reflecting on your own childhood to see what style of parenting you were exposed to. Here are some of the combinations: negligent father, permissive mother; dominant father, negligent mother; dominant father, dominant mother (lots of conflict), and so forth.

Responsible Parenting Is Loving

Responsible parents are both authoritative (not *authoritarian*) and positive in approach. They believe that parents have the right to be leaders in the family, but do not falter when the children may raise objections to the direction. This kind of home usually welcomes other children, and the parents may well be popular listeners to some of their children's friends at various ages. How does this happen? Mostly through hard work and time for love to develop.

Loving parenting means honesty with yourself and your children as they grow. Your child can't admit a mistake if you don't model that behavior for him. He can't take a risk unless he's seen your example. Responsible parenting is being willing to fail, but not to play it safe. The aim is high and the effort is great; the results are therefore better than they might otherwise have been.

Loving children is not easy. When you feel angry about the responsibilities of parenting, express that anger to each other or to a friend. In some cases you may need to express your frustration to your children. As you do, make sure you express your feelings and take the responsibility for them—don't blame your children for the way you feel or act. *Example:* A blaming parent heaps on the guilt by saying to his child, "You made me mad," or "If it weren't for you, I wouldn't feel this way." Neither of those is true! The loving parent admits his feelings by saying "I am angry." Or, "I'm upset with these circumstances." Using the freedom to express your feelings openly provides a secure platform for your child when he must deal with his own anger and disappointment.

Here are four major characteristics of responsible parents:

1. *The underlying tone is honesty, not deceptiveness.* Dealing with yourself and your circumstances openly teaches your children that you will deal fairly with them. Denying the reality of feelings or events undermines their confidence in you and models dishonest reactions as the style to employ.

2. *The style is one of awareness rather than insensitivity.* In this model, parenting flows from within. The parent is aware of himself and therefore aware of his children's needs. Family life can be built on a feeling level, rather than just a functional level. In this kind of relationship, tasks are important, but always secondary to people.

3. *The parents offer freedom rather than dominance.* Privileges are given to children commensurate with age and ability, but the stance remains an encouragement to move toward greater self-responsibility for each member of the family. Parents see themselves as partners in the growth process of

their children, rather than competitors between themselves or their offspring.

4. *The atmosphere is based on trust rather than suspicion.* Discouraged parents often develop cynicism in dealing with their children. They find themselves feeling, "I've got to outmanipulate these kids; control or be controlled." The responsible parent enjoys his children more because he not only trusts them and develops their trust, but he encourages them to trust others by his example.

The bottom line comes out with the parent assisting the child to become all that he can be. The beauty of that process is that the parent's deepest needs are most fully met as the child grows into his potential.

Some parents usually ask me how one can assume such a stance. "Don't children take advantage of our support and walk on us?" is a rather familiar question. The answer is, only if we lie down. Responsible parenting is the balance between the best of parental skills and the needs of children. Our children need *both* control and support to grow up whole. Control without support produces robots or rebels; neither excites the heart of a parent. Support without control results in delinquents or dropouts, at the extremes. A total approach to the parenting process—awareness, honesty, trust, and freedom—demands the most of each parent and each child.

Loving children means helping them to break the restrictions that would keep them from their own development and instilling in them the internal limits they choose for personal growth and fulfillment.

SEVEN

Develop Your Philosophy Positively

"Breed is stronger than pasture."

George Eliot

A patient complaining to his psychiatrist about being depressed was asked, "Did your depression develop suddenly, or was it the natural result of marrying and having children?" We joke about the pressures of parenting because none of us escape its frustrations and responsibilities, but all parents have a common goal: to help their children grow up to be healthy, mature people. The question is, how do they do it?

Jesus, when asked what His purpose on earth was, contrasted Himself to a thief who comes to kill and destroy and compared Himself to a shepherd who comes to give full life. The shepherding model may well be the proper analogy for responsible parenting. We parents are called on to guide our children through the wilderness of growing up, into the pastures of fulfillment and maturity. There are many dangers and temptations for us and our children as we fulfill this obligation.

Look at some of the available ways of parenting, each one containing truth, but none complete in itself:

The Natural Process

The hedonistic parent basically depends on the pleasure principle. He teaches his child that personal pleasure is the ultimate test of successful living. "What feels good is what you want to do in life. Let nature take its course . . . the survival of the fittest brings happiness." Responsibility is to yourself alone.

The Social Process

Other parents teach their children the value of other people. "Let your friends guide you to what is best, as we have done. Do what is expected of you, and people will like you—that's the way to get along in the world and be happy." The goal is to be appreciated by or respected by other people. Responsibility is to others.

The Moral Process

Some parents instill healthy consciences in their children. They value the proper and institutional causes in life. "Let your conscience be your guide, and do your duty." Responsibility is to the common good of the group, whether it's a nation, club, church, or family.

The Rational Process

Education seems to be the ultimate goal for some parents. The mind is a terrible thing to waste, but reason may not be the only savior of children. These parents want intelligent, capable, and rational children who can think through issues and arrive at correct solutions to human problems. Responsibility is to clear rational process.

Develop Your Philosophy Positively

The Emotional Level

"Trust your heart, your deep feelings," is the advice of emotional parenting. "Be honest, even if it is painful. Do what you feel is right, deep within you." The Socratic wisdom of "Know thyself" has been wed to Shakespeare's "To thine own self be true, and it must follow, as the night the day, thou canst not then be false to any man." Responsibility in this system is to the integrity of the self, the feeling level of life.

All five of these value systems provide certain benefits to their followers, but responsible parenting will demand more than any of these can offer alone. Some have suggested that the spiritual answer is the one.

The Spiritual Process

"Depend on God and His guidance, and everything will work out right for you," says the spiritually inclined parent. "Have faith, trust in God. Even if life has mysteries, we believe that in eternity, we'll understand the answers."

None of these ideas by itself produces a balanced life. If parents are to help their children discover the fullness of life, the approach must be an integrative one, drawing from all the philosophies mentioned above. Responsible parenting is integrative processing.

Seven Steps to Responsible Parenting

In my book, *Being Up in a Down World,* I listed the seven steps of personal growth. An application of these to the parenting process seems appropriate. They are:

Awareness
Articulation

Action
Actualization
Assessment
Affirmation
Achievement

The responsible parent not only develops his own personal growth through guidelines like these, he also helps his child learn to mature through this process.

Awareness Insight into our children is the result of observing, listening, and hearing them. In the early years, our insights must be built on our knowledge and skills as well as our nonverbal sensitivity to the child. As the child's verbal skills develop, his awareness of our insight into ourselves will be gained by hearing us talk about our feelings and attitudes, especially in response to his curiosity about everything. The more we encourage that process, the more aware of the world he will become; the more we discourage it, the less creative he is likely to be. He is also likely to develop inward feelings of awareness, but will not feel the freedom to share them with his parents.

Articulation In order for us to trust our insights, we must reality test them with others. Your child needs this opportunity to check out his feelings and ideas by expressing them freely. They are the verbalizing of his awareness of the world. Sometimes the only word he seems to know is *why*. Yet, the process of forming ideas into words and sharing those, particularly with parents, is essential to psychological growth. As parents frame and reframe their own ideas with their children, they predispose them to an open verbal exchange in later life.

Action Growth is begun in the conceptualizing and speaking of reality, but it is best confirmed by some step of action. The journey of a thousand miles still begins with a single step. Parenting in a responsible fashion requires that we encourage our children to incorporate their words into behavior. Small steps at first lead to greater involvement in the future. Acting on what I say makes the growth process concrete for both me and my child.

Actualization Habitualization develops as the parent and child mature together. Confirming the first step of action and giving support to that process, the parent assists his child in forming good habits throughout life. He plays a significant role of reinforcing in his child the positives or negatives he chooses or allows within the framework of their relationship. For the parent, actualization means continuing a process of growth and cooperation with the child's development of his own patterns of growth and reinforcement.

Assessment A necessary but sometimes difficult part of growth is the evaluation phase. To reality test for myself is difficult, and to be objective about my child also demands great objectivity. Teaching that skill requires patient and firm discipline within myself. The delicate balance between rating myself too easily and being overly critical of my faults requires extreme sensitivity to reality rather than fantasy. Seeing things as they really are does not come easily. Most parents allow themselves not only to filter their views of personal behavior, but to screen out the negatives they witness in their children. Realistic evaluation is a necessity for growth and positive parenting.

Affirmation When my evaluation helps me decide that a level of growth is basically positive, affirmation of that process comes next. It takes twenty-one days to establish a physical habit and longer to reinforce an emotional change. Parents have the opportunity (through praise and support) to help the child establish a feeling or a habit as a buttress against failure. What is regularly bolstered in my emotional experience becomes a foundation piece of living.

Achievement   The zenith of growth is arriving at the goal of your efforts. Change from something to something else is that accomplishment. Not only must the responsible parent seek new developments in his own growth, but he also must strengthen his child in the quest for new dimensions of living.

The Integrative Process

Positive parenting is the result of integrating all of life. Living truth cannot be encapsulated in any single system; its reality is expressed through a personality. I have the opportunity not only of assimilating ideas and understandings about my world into a workable balance for myself, but as a parent, I must also distill from those experiences the key ingredients of life and share them with my children. Making the process personal requires creativity from me.

Helen Hunt Jackson said, "The parent who creates and sustains a home, and under whose hands children grow to be strong and pure men and women is a creator second only to God." That challenge invites parents to discover the balance between personal needs and the child's needs. Positive parenting is not losing yourself in your children, but finding *more of yourself* through child rearing. Responsible parenting makes the adult a better person because of the experience of guiding the child. When two parents fully share the challenge, a better marriage is the result.

Parenting can, however, put stress on marriage. Don't lose your marriage in the responsibility of parenthood.

EIGHT

Ground Your Family Faithfully

Reverence for God
gives a man deep strength;
his children have a place
of refuge and security.
Proverbs 14:26 TLB

The process of responsible parenting is the cement that holds the family together. Parents, however, are not the foundation of the family; its institutional roots are ancient. Like the existence of God, the family is assumed in the biblical tradition. The family does not exist as an expression of its faith; its faith supports the family in its function.

The nature of the family is grounded in the nature of God—we call it His fatherhood. This ancient rooting of the family makes it our first institution, long before the church or school. Pope Leo XIII once said: "The family was ordained of God in order that children might be trained up for Himself; it was before the church." Margaret Mead, the late anthropologist, noted: "All the attempts in human history to eradicate the family have failed. The family will change form and lifestyle, but it is here to stay." That theological and philosophical underpinning remains important because it permeates and assures us as parents that we will survive.

The family—and therefore the parenting process—remains under attack. The communists would replace parents with the state; homosexuals want to redefine the family ethic to minimize not only biology, but also the emotional importance of heterosexual parenting roles; and the economic stress of this age places such burdens on parents that much of the teaching and guidance is left to paid professionals in education, psychology, therapy, and recreational fields. Yet the family remains the most influential institution on earth, even if it is apparently outmanned by the other systems of power. The greatest influence on your self-esteem, your development as a unique individual, still comes from your family. Who you are is determined in large measure by the influence of the home in which you grew up. For many, that included the extended input of relatives such as grandparents, uncles, aunts, and other assorted relatives. A friend of mine jokes that success is relative—the more success, the more relatives! Nothing is the butt of jokes like the family, yet nothing affects us so significantly.

Parents have the opportunity to establish a mini-nation, in which each child is an ambassador-at-large representing the kingdom. That not only gives parents a major responsibility, but also provides a great opportunity for personal extension of values and convictions. I began very early with my children to use the "emotional coat of arms" theory. In heraldry, the knight wore a symbol of his clan or family, and often the coat of arms was displayed before the castle or home. I taught my sons and daughter that the name Kilgore was important. When they left home, instead of saying, "Be a good boy [or girl]," I often left them with,

"Remember what your name is." They represented the Kilgore family. I'm on the fortunate side of parenting now, where I can begin to see those ideas taking root and bearing evidence in their adult lives.

Children don't always comprehend the total picture. Dr. Robert Schuller tells of an incident in his son's life in which, at five years of age, he tried to represent the family's values to a guest. On the way home from the airport they ran out of gas, and Schuller began to walk to the service station. Shortly after he left, the older man in the car with Schuller's son pulled a cigar from his pocket and began to smoke. Little Bob had heard many times about the dangers of smoking and that it was linked to cancer. In childlike honesty, he said to the man, "You shouldn't do that, you'll get a horrible disease." A bit struck, the gentleman asked, "What disease is that, Son?" Undaunted, the little boy blurted out, "Diarrhea." Obviously, the child didn't get all the facts, but he had the right idea.

The family not only gives the parent the opportunity to implant values in the child, but provides the one place where he can be accepted with total honesty, in spite of all his idiosyncratic quirks. The family is like a group-therapy experience. For the last eighteen years I have professionally led groups through my counseling center. I have been struck numerous times by this common sentiment that group members have expressed to one another: "You are like a family to me, at least the way I'd like my family to be." That sense of being accepted the way I am feels like a family atmosphere to the members of a group. Parenting is the process through which that tone can be set in a home. How this is done may vary from family to family.

One thermostat of the family's interaction can be the dinner table. In America, one of the family tragedies is that life becomes so hectic and at times disjointed that many families miss the opportunity of sitting at the table with one another. Leslie Parrot, in the book *Easy to Live With*, describes four kinds of dinner conversations:

1. *Monosyllabic terseness.* The dinner table becomes a self-service fuel center where you fill your tank and move on. Six words characterize the exchanges: *more, yes, salt, pepper, please,* and *thanks.*

2. *Family discipline and correction.* The main course served is criticism. Usually the family "black sheep" is roasted and the dinner often ends with an early exit by one of the family members, usually accompanied by a slammed door.

3. *Family protection and pride.* The outside evils of the world or the neighbors are usually reviewed, engendering a kind of Pharisaism, "I'm glad we're not like them."

4. *A better level is the table exchange which centers around positive comments about people and things.* Very few dinner conversations rise to the level of social or political ideas.

Rarely do people share personal feelings and a sense of intimacy over the mealtime experience. However, one of the characteristics of intimates is that they often linger at the table, enjoying sharing with one another. The family may engender the same closeness when all members, including parents, are encouraged to share themselves in a relaxed and casual way.

Reflect on your own mealtime experiences. Is the family thermostat set on positive or negative?

The most important foundation a child may receive, both in feeling tone and in example, comes from the parenting process. Parents discover that the hardest place to practice honesty is in the home. Contrast these two vignettes from the lives of well-known Americans.

General Patton was invited to give a speech on Armistice

Day when his son George was a senior in high school. The principal was somewhat concerned about Patton's candor and salty language. "Don't worry," Patton assured the principal, "I know how to talk to young men." He gave an inspiring address. Following the ceremonies, there was a football game in which his son played end. With his team behind 6-0, George ran into the end zone near the end of the game. The quarterback threw him a long pass at the goal line. He had the ball in his hands, but dropped it. His father stormed out of the stands and castigated his son with all the unexpurgated Anglo-Saxon phrases he knew. With his own family, he failed to inspire.

A personal friend of Norman Vincent Peale tells a different story. Peale was in the midst of an important business conference when his secretary buzzed him. "Excuse me," he said, and spent almost fifteen minutes listening on the phone before saying to his daughter, "I know you're disappointed at losing the election, Honey, but your mother and I are proud of you. We love you and think you are the most beautiful girl in the world." His daughter was fifteen and had lost a class election. No one witnessed the scene except the visitor in Peale's office.

Positive parenting is often a private experience that no one knows about, except you and your child. Survival in the emotionally draining world of parental responsibility demands a clear concept from us as parents and the conviction that it will be worth the effort we have exerted. That commitment is the foundation for successful parenting.

NINE

Lead Your Family Effectively

"The child is the father of the man."
William Wordsworth

The most successful parents I know have learned how to model an attractive life-style for their children. That's parental leadership. The same basic principles for success in the rest of life work at home, if we apply them within the family perspective. Fathers should have the edge on mothers in most cases, because of their greater experience in the marketplace of life, but that is the result of exposure, not because they are male. In my experience, however, many men fail to utilize what they know works at the office when they come home.

Charles and his family came to see me some years ago. He was an extremely successful businessman. He appeared to have the Midas touch when it came to money. Susan was a very traditional woman who loved having babies and being involved in community activities. When their children were small, they had the usual time pressures and couple misunderstandings, but as the children grew older, they sensed more serious difficulties. The oldest girl was caught with some drugs and began having some unusual difficulties at school. Even though Carrie was fourteen, I had them come for evaluations as a family.

The variety of problems in the family cannot be discussed here, but one of the early discoveries we made was that Charles used an entirely different system of leadership at home than he did at work. His treatment of employees was very sensitive. He motivated people by encouraging them to find new ways to approach their professional and personal challenges. But when he came home, he lapsed into a dictatorial position. Susan had adapted somewhat, but Carrie refused and began to rebel. For Charles, that meant he needed to come down harder on her, but he had begun to feel defeated in that relationship.

He complained that too many other people influenced his children. "How can I get my daughter to do right in the face of television, magazines, and her lousy friends?" he asked. Is it possible for us to teach our values to our children? The answer is a confident yes. Here are some suggestions:

1. *Utilize the position of parent well.* In spite of the fact that our children rebel against some of our ideas, we have the closest place from which to teach—if we use it. Home is where a child can ask questions that he might be afraid to ask anywhere else. Parents have the intimate setting of the home, where quiet, nonpublic discussions can take place.

2. *Encourage your child to ask any question.* Even if you don't know the answer, when you admit that and help him seek the information, you will enhance your child's confidence in you. Our children are hurt more by what they don't know than by what they understand. Be open to any inquiry your child brings. "I don't know, but we'll find out together" is always an acceptable answer.

3. *Share your values openly with your children.* All of us have experiences from which we have learned. Each parent needs to say what he has been taught and why he believes it. Forget the "when I was your age" qualifications, and simply tell your child how you learned your important lessons in life. He will respect that and appreciate your personal candor.

4. *Model your values before your children.* The ancient Proverb says "Train a child in the right way, and when he is old, he will follow it" (*see* Proverbs 22:6). What your child sees you do is believable. Take him with you to shop, to worship, to visit friends, and to play, so that he can observe the way you live what you believe.

5. *Introduce your child to other good role models.* Discover the people who share your views and ideals, and help your child know them. A scout leader, a coach, a teacher, or a minister may be a vital asset in helping you influence your children positively.

Responsible parenting means teaching my children who I am and what I believe first. They will then have a basis for their own decision making in the future.

Modeling as a parent means demonstrating your abilities with encouragement. What we say is often not as important as how we say it as leaders in the family. I believe encouragement is the key to change in the behavior of most of our children. The dictatorial stance is as ineffective as nagging.

"How will I ever get some sense through that thick skull of yours?" the father screamed at the son sitting across the room. The boy was a master of the nonverbal, staring at his father, then shrugging his shoulders as if to say, "Don't bother me, Dad." If that scene occurred only infrequently, I would not call it to your attention. Unfortunately, it is repeated far too often between parents and teenagers.

Children rarely become what we nag them about; they

more often develop where our encouragement leads them. Watch a good teacher at work in a classroom. That teacher's best energies are applied encouraging the students to learn, infusing them with excitement about new frontiers of intellectual curiosity and the limitless boundaries of their own curiosity. Poor teachers nag. Good teachers encourage. Parents can be good or bad teachers. Encouragement is the key.

A father nagged his son about his poor judgment and bad behavior, but there was no change. He decided to try a different approach. He had a talk with himself and deliberately began to encourage his son toward more acceptable behavior. Initially there was only a slight change, but the more consistent he became, the greater the improvement in his son's responses. Before long the son began asking for his father's help, whereas he had previously been ignoring his father's advice. When I asked the young man what made the change, he said something very interesting: "When my Dad is being nice to me, I like having him around. If he's a grouch, I just ignore him." He didn't use the word *encouragement*, but he recognized what it felt like.

Try this on for size in your family. Encourage your child as much as you can for thirty days. Be positive in your attitudes. Praise him wherever possible. You'll be surprised at the outcome. It may just be the touch your child needs.

Another dimension of parental leadership is perspective. An effective leader in any field attempts to see things through the eyes of those he leads. He needs that perspective in order to make the most challenging decisions. How one gains that point of view can be interesting.

A few years ago in working with a family in conflict, I realized that the father just would not or could not understand what his little boy was trying to say. He couldn't see the world from the same point of view. One day when they came into the office, I asked the father to get down on his knees and stay there for a while. I asked his son to stand next to him while they talked for a few minutes. For the first time, the father was looking up to his son and the son was looking down to his father. At the end of the session, the father said, "This was a waste of time." In a few days, however, he called to make another appointment. What he said was important: "I never realized what the world looked like from the belt-buckle level."

Families have the best understanding—at least they have the best opportunity to be understanding—of the perspective each member has on the world. A teenager said to me, "My Dad is a pain in the neck." I discovered that his father was quite tall and towered over him when he corrected him. No wonder his neck hurt, and the association was made.

Try seeing the world from the perspective of the other members of your family. You don't have to get on your knees physically, although that sometimes helps. Listen to the way they describe things—see the world through their eyes today. You may get a different point of view.

Too many of us as parents function like the T-shirt seen in the store window: "There they go, and I must hurry, for I am their leader." I'm ready for a new surge of parental leadership in our world. We need it here in America especially. Parents are the key influence in their children's lives. No one doubts that, but my experience says that we are willing for it to happen more by accident than direction.

People feel good about themselves as parents when they have a plan for sharing with their children and when they carry that plan out effectively. I believe it starts in the pre-parenting process and continues right through the early phases of maturing adulthood. Leader parents do not fall into the trap of permissiveness; they demonstrate engaging lives for their children.

A final note about leader parents: You are not up for election. You have a lifelong position that comes with conception and birth. The question you face is not "Will I be a popular parent?" but "Will I be effective in communicating my goals and values to my children?" Good parental leadership listens to the needs and responds to the child. If your child does not respond immediately with your intended results, be patient enough with yourself to allow that promised success to arrive: "Train up a child in the way he should go: and when he is old, he will not depart from it" (Proverbs 22:6). Our job as parents is to do the training and wait expectantly for the outcome.

PART THREE

Parenting Process

"The words that a father speaks to his children in the privacy of home are not heard by the world, but, as in whispering-galleries, they are clearly heard at the end and by posterity."

Jean Paul Richter

TEN

The Growing Parent

**"Paternity is a career imposed
on you without an inquiry into
your fitness."**
Adlai E. Stevenson

The true meaning of responsibility in life often eludes us.
We try to be responsible for the things we really can't accept responsibility for, and often feel most guilty about not
doing the things for which we are really most responsible.
This concept can be most difficult to define, but it is extremely important to parental survival.

Look at Marge. She is an extremely competent executive
who has risen to the top in her company. She functions
beautifully, or as she puts it, "I'm the best female machine
you'll ever see. I'm like the oil in my company's engine. I
make things go smoothly. It's when I get home that I feel so
miserable. I'm in constant conflict with my kids."

She wasn't lying. When I saw the children, they attested
to the turmoil, but blamed it on their mother's job. She had
three children—seventeen, fourteen, and nine. The girls
were seventeen and nine. Marge was overwhelmed by the

lack of dependability in her teenagers. The more we talked together, the more it became clear that she had been a very "good" mother, especially in the grade-school years. She stayed home and took care of their needs until she became a widow four years ago. She was forced to return to the work force and found a job where her personality and the company's needs fit beautifully. She was now vice-president in charge of customer service. "That's a glorified trouble-shooter," she explained. She really was a good problem solver, but it didn't seem to work at home. "Everybody depends on me at work," she complained. "I can't depend on Michelle and Jack at all. Cynthia isn't much difficulty, but she's not a teenager yet."

Marge wanted to have responsible children, but it appeared that she was getting irresponsibility and rebellion. The contrast between her success at work and her failure (by her standards) at home was baffling, until Marge began to look at her needs as a parent. She needed to be needed at home so much that she did everything for her children, too. She was still vice-president for customer service to them. But inwardly she felt used and cheated by their lack of participation in the home chores and responsibilities.

We decided to work out a new system for the home. The children were to be responsible for their own rooms and assigned tasks. Marge was only to help if they asked for help and she could feel justified in what was requested. A chart was made to show each person's assignment, and the children agreed to share the load. The first week nothing worked, and Marge was back in my office alone.

"How much can you really do for your children, Marge?" I asked.

"Almost anything they need," she responded.

"That's the problem. You won't let them take responsibility, so they don't." It sounded harsh, but I began to get through to her. She agreed not to sabotage the plan. Six months have passed now. Things aren't perfect, but they are improved. Marge is finding the change more difficult than her teenagers, especially Jack, who is now ironing his own shirts and jeans.

What Marge's resistance illustrates is our vulnerability as parents. We think we are totally answerable for our children's wants and needs. If we position ourselves this way, our children will take advantage of us. The outcome can be resentment that we lived our lives for them only to find that they will not live for us in exchange. Marge felt good about her work because she was rewarded for her sacrifice financially and with expressed appreciation. Her work at home was taken for granted by the children.

Children must learn to appreciate the parent through verbal and nonverbal direction. The parent who affirms himself as a person will be ready for the teenage transition; he can become an adult friend to his child. The parent who expresses doubts and fears and allows his child to be demanding of him sets himself up for conflict and frustration. A parent who is a person first survives. Look at these three principles for meaningful accomplishment as a parent.

Be Yourself!

Before you write me off as just another self-help psychologist talking about parenting, face this crucial idea. Most parental "failures" are defined by external models or expectations. Who decides whether you are handling parenting well? your spouse? your own parents? your children? Now you see the emphasis—*you* are the ultimate judge, because you have the final responsibility. No one else can fail for you, but no one else can succeed for you. You are the best at being who you are; no one else can be you as a parent.

The major frustration of parents is the uneasy feeling that they might not be doing enough for their children. Inwardly we compare ourselves to our parents, to the unexamined ideas we have about other parents we know, and to our own best moments in the parenting process.

Comparisons to our own parents can be reassuring if we felt that our parents did not spend enough time, didn't show enough affection, and so forth. If we had great parents, however, then the comparison may be negative. When we look at others' children and the way they behave as a gauge of our own parenting, the assumptions can also be misleading. Too many parents reflect on the mountaintop emotional times with their children and have trouble balancing the scales when they are in the valleys of distance and dissatisfaction.

To be yourself as a parent begins with knowing yourself the best you can. In much the same manner as you examined your marriage in chapter one, look at your development as a person who has become a parent. Think back on the kind of parenting you have received, both from your real parents and the other parent figures in your life. As you consider these, what are the most pleasant memories you recall? When did you feel most comforted and protected as a child? When did you feel most supported in your steps to independence? These memories constitute your bank of expectations, or hopes for yourself as a parent. The realistic examination of your abilities determines how well you can succeed in fulfilling those goals. You cannot relive someone else's pattern as a parent. You can be yourself.

Manage Yourself!

Parenting is a process—a changing, developing relationship between you and your child over a period of years. The major functional task is management of the relationship during the reversal from one extreme to the other. The parent is totally responsible and in control while the child is young and dependent. Through the turbulent teenage years, the parent transfers control and responsibility until, hopefully, the young adult can manage for himself. Since most of the negotiations revolve around feelings and self-esteem, this management transfer can be more demanding than any comparable transaction, such as management-labor negotiations.

Some parents are much more effective at certain stages of the process than others. The father who comfortably plays with his infant daughter may have more anxiety about her emerging role as a woman. Mothers whose little boys have been extremely affectionate may feel rejected by their teenagers, who seem to be less comfortable with hugs and kisses, especially with Mom! Of course, children make unrealistic and childish demands on us during this process. A television commercial some years ago showed a little boy making his favorite lunch to take with him when he ran away from home. As he put the sandwiches in the bag, he turned to his mother and said, "Aren't you going to drive me?" Humorous, but illustrative.

Managing yourself as a parent means fulfilling your needs as well as those of your child. That sounds easy, but multiplies stress in parents immeasurably. The "nice" parent sacrifices so that his child can have what he wants, but he may eventually begin to ask when his own turn comes. Nearly 40 percent of middle-aged parents having affairs have told me that one of the factors was finding a situation where "I could be myself." As one mother of four put it about her romantic interest, "He seems to listen and love me for what I am. My husband and children give me the old 'what have you done for me lately?' response."

That reaction to family stress is a reflection of poor self-management. My first responsibility is to manage me. I'll then be a better husband, parent, employee, and so forth in the various roles I fulfill. An essential part of being myself is managing my personal resources in parenting, as well as the other demands of my life. Time becomes an important factor. A parent needs time for himself for relaxation, recreation, renewal, and recharging of the intellectual, emotional, and spiritual generators of his life. As I accept the responsibility for my own time management as a parent, I model for my children how they can manage themselves. If I fail to be a good self-manager, they are likely to develop poor patterns, too.

Poor self-management reflects a lack of self-esteem. I need to be able to identify my needs and be assertive about having them fulfilled, without failing others or abusing their rights. Disappointing my child by not fulfilling his expectations may be uncomfortable, but as a parent I recognize that I can't fulfill all his wishes. What I promise or negotiate with my child has great significance, but I need to manage the other expectations and demands he may have in the light of my own needs and resources.

Gerald appeared to be a very successful professional person. His finely tailored three-piece suit and expensive shoes seemed his natural dress for the business day. I met him at a Rotary Club speaking engagement. He called later for an appointment. "I'll get right to the point, Jim," he said in a no-nonsense style. "I'm just not sure I can handle all the demands of my life, particularly those from my family. I'm really seriously considering moving out for a while. I don't think I want a divorce, and I know I love my kids, but I don't know how much more pressure I can take." As we explored his situation, he unfolded some common elements: the successful business career, a somewhat demanding and socially climbing wife, and three apparently normal boys at home. Having grown up with a professional father tending toward workaholism, he had promised himself more time with his children. His wife was more social and less athletic and was involved with the sons' athletic programs minimally. She was quite critical of his lack of time with his sons. Business was going very well, but "self-employed people work long hours" as he described it. His frustration was evident. As we worked together, Gerald began to recall some of his own family background. His wife occasionally sounded like his own mother; the things she said reminded him of his youthful pledges to spend time with his own children. He felt great pride in his professional accomplishments, but the guilt he experienced about homelife troubled him.

His problem was self-management. We talked about his expectations and discussed a plan for more time off from work, as well as some ideas about better time use there. We planned some experiments for him in personal recreation, as well as time for his wife and boys. In addition, we outlined some issues he needed to talk over with his wife and some listening exercises to be done with his sons. Three weeks passed before he came again. When I asked how he had done, he said, "Things really aren't much different in some ways, but I feel a whole lot better. I think I'm in charge of my life again." What he described let me know that many changes had been made that contributed to his positive feelings of self-esteem. Being in charge was more fun than being under pressure.

Enjoy Yourself!

The third principle for meaningful parental accomplishment is to enjoy your parenting. Accept parenthood as a responsibility, but not as a burden. Uptight children are usually the result of uptight parents; being at ease with your children conditions them to relax. Besides the "adult" play in your life, take advantage of the opportunity to play with your child. No man can parent his biological child who cannot be kind to the emotional child within himself.

To be childlike doesn't imply irresponsible behavior. Discovering the ecstasy, wonder, and beauty of the world can be childlike. Not taking yourself so seriously is childlike. Risking your curiosity and not knowing something are properties of childlikeness. Much of what we laugh about with our children is their utter abandon to experiences of delight—the smiles, giggles, wide eyes, and breathlessness. Parents need to cherish moments like that for themselves. Sometimes, through shared reflections of the past, parents stimulate the childlikeness in each other. Occasionally the experience comes through reliving a childhood experience of your own by sharing it with your children. However it happens, hold those precious times like rare jewels.

Mark and Cheryl were in their early thirties, with a boy of twelve and a girl of ten. The ten-year-old was not doing well in school. I asked to see the whole family. After several visits, Melissa, the daughter, with a little coaxing, asked her mother what school was like for her. In an almost embarrassed style, Cheryl began to share some of her experiences. Then Mark told about his fifth-grade memories. Soon the family and I were laughing about the incidents. I suggested as a follow-up to our session that they repeat this kind of sharing the following Sunday night. Two weeks later the teacher called to say that Melissa's attitude, if not her average, had improved considerably. She was most impressed by Melissa's new relationships with her fellow students and the way she had shared in social times, telling stories about her parents' experiences in school.

Mark and Cheryl had been serious about parenting, almost muting their own good sense of humor for the last ten or twelve years. Soon they left family therapy, but with a new sense of family sharing and happiness. If I were a mechanic, I would describe my work with them as fine tuning, rather than a major overhaul. But I, too, enjoy the smooth sounds of the engine. Their family looked more relaxed the last time I saw them.

Parents succeed when these simple ideas are put into practice: Be yourself, manage yourself, and enjoy yourself. When you really live for yourself, you teach your children how to live for themselves, too. If you don't assert yourself, prepare for the battleground where some parents don't survive emotionally. It's called the teen years—the twixt twelve and twenty test!

ELEVEN

Teens
Are Tests

"If a child annoys you, quiet him by brushing his hair. If this doesn't work, use the other side of the brush on the other end of the child."

Anonymous

I have now completed the course. My youngest child is past twenty. I write this book not with the air of superiority, but a prayer of gratitude. So far, I have three magnificent children and an exceptional partner in life! I don't dislike teenagers—in fact, I enjoy other people's teens a great deal. This chapter is not a diatribe against the transition from twelve to twenty, but a resource to help other parents survive and feel good about themselves while they do.

The battle of wills does not begin when your child turns thirteen; you just can't miss it then. He may be as big as you are by that time. She is physically becoming a woman, even if you sometimes think maturity is developing everywhere except the brain. More freedom is given and demanded in those years. But the most significant change may be emergence of peer-group pressure. "Everybody else" becomes the focal point of almost any defense you'll hear from those children you used to guide. They may not say it; they may wear it, style it, or listen to it. Their clothes, their hair, and their stereos reflect the invasion of the peer group.

Some parents suppress the individuality of their children, as well as their need to be accepted. Early in the "everybody else" battles, I told mine that I was glad they were different; I loved having unique children. But they didn't like being different, so we had to work out some compromises.

A parenthesis here: You can't compromise your values as a parent. There are some lines over which you will not step. Be clear and stick to your guns over these issues. I'm not talking about having no rules when I say compromise. A compromise is an understanding. Literally, compromise means "to come to promise" (Latin: *compromitere*). It is the result of talking about and understanding something new, achieving a more significant level of trust.

How can you compromise? First decide what is really important to you. During the 1960s, parents and teenagers argued a good deal about the length of hair, particularly with the male population. Hair became a symbol of protest. A good deal more than hair was at stake in the protest movement, which was really a rebellion against most forms of the establishment. It may have been easier to fight over the length of the teenager's hair than to address the weightier issues involved.

What are your critical points of commitment in life? If it is your faith, make that clear to your children (hopefully before they become teens). How is that important reality to be handled? If it is a family custom for everyone to worship on Sunday, be explicit. You cannot make them believe, but you can require their exposure while you have primary responsibility.

If your commitment to marriage is significant, that, too, needs to be known. How is it to be applied? Be clear that two friends of the opposite sex may be welcomed as overnight guests in separate bedrooms. Don't back off your principle, no matter how much you are challenged or badgered.

But find some room for compromise when lesser issues emerge. It may be the dirty-room issue. Instead of an unending battle over the cleanliness of her room, close the door. As long as she's decent and clean (not necessarily dressed the way you wish) go easy on that confrontation. Save your energy for the important bouts. You'll need it!

Let's not forget the peer group. Your teens have some models and some confidants you may not even know. Fight back; form your own peer group. Parent power groups, or whatever title the parent-support program assumes, are needed as places for dialogue and exchange. Many parents have learned through the programs established to fight drugs and drug abuse. The same basic ingredients suggested for the preparenting program can be used for the parent-support program. You can invite one couple to discuss common parenting problems, or form a group. In any case, if you are the instigator, some parent with less courage will thank you. Parents need one another, and most of the problems have common roots. Some difficulties are much more acute than others and therefore require more extreme responses. I have seen the parents of apparently well-behaved kids learn from those whose children have had trouble with the law. Many other youthful offenses may have been avoided by these kinds of exchange.

Parent Power

The more docile among us may even shrink from the word *power*. The sound of black power, lib power, or gray power may be too closely associated. This base is not political. Parents don't need to march on Washington; they merely need to support one another! All parents don't need to band together in a national organization; the basic need is for parents in a common area with similar needs to share their ideas and feelings.

Similar interests help. The parents of a given church group or those of the same high school or a particular neighborhood may meet to discuss their common needs. Sometimes it happens informally at the neighborhood block party or around the community swimming pool. It may begin in the couples' Sunday school class. Wherever it starts, parent power has as its objective strengthening the hands of parents in dealing with their teenagers.

Your son may say that all the other boys use the family car on Saturday nights. Check it out with the fathers you know. Talk about the curfew hours other parents have. You may not decide to change yours. The principle of parent power is information, not conformity. Parents should not try to be like other parents, but at least know what worked for them.

Familiar Fights

Conflicts take on the specific character and quality of each family, but there are some common experiences worth noting. Here are three typical responses you may hear from your children.

Blackmail Almost all parents at one time or another will hear the emotional blackmail of "If you really loved me . . ."

or "You must not love me, or you wouldn't be so mean." Usually this is a way to try to beat the parent down after a decision has been made. The teenager may not be sure the decision is firm or may simply be reflecting hostility or anger.

This retort can be whined through tears, which is more effective on fathers. It is the style of a child who feels like a martyr, but the end result is to increase the parents' guilt or anxiety. "How could you do this to me?" sounds like the parental response, but the message is the same. Another blackmailing style is the belligerent accusation. The sledge-hammer words are hurled at the parent, in order to destroy his defenses. The teen reasons that if he can make you feel bad enough, you'll change your mind about the decision.

Logical deduction Some teens are experts at the "fair-ness" doctrine. "Do you really think that's fair?" they will ask with incredulity. Or the accusation is made that your assumption is wrong. "How could you think that about me?" one teenager screams, while another questions whether or not you have really thought your position through carefully.

Shoulder slang One of the most common experiences of parents is the nonverbal response that comes when a teen is confronted or caught in a situation. The shoulders are raised and lowered, while the eyes avoid contact. If words are spoken, they are usually, "I don't know" or "I forgot." Occasionally a teen will say, "I didn't think . . . ," to which many parents would say, "Amen!"

I was leading a parent-teen conference in a local church recently when a mother said to me at a break, "These kids here are terrific; it's mine that are hard to love." Many young people feel much the same about their parents. The

Los Angeles Times syndicate carried this line: "To love the world is no big chore. It's that miserable guy next door who is the problem."

Parent power is important for the sake of your teens. They look to you for the measure of strength, for an example of conviction, even when they decide to disagree and reject it. It's better for your teenagers to know what your values are and to decide differently for themselves than to wonder how you felt about something. Your survival—with strength—is vital to their future lives.

TWELVE

Family Communication Skills

"The family is a unit composed not only of children, but of men, women, an occasional animal, and the common cold."
Ogden Nash

The Family Conference

For nearly two decades now, I've been teaching parents and children to use a basic technique—the family conference. Every family needs a vehicle through which its members can communicate, and the family conference has become that useful tool for many families. If it is to be effective, certain basic ground rules need to be established. Try some of these on for size in your family setting:

1. *The time for meeting must be established at a regular interval*—weekly, biweekly, monthly, and so forth. The time selected should be as congenial to all of the family members as possible. Don't expect to be successful if you schedule the family meeting first thing on Monday morning, when everyone is preparing for the new work week, school assign-

ments, and rushing to get dressed. Late Sunday afternoon or evening has proven to be useful to many families. The calendar for the coming week's activities can be reviewed and agreements reached for the responsibilities to be accepted. Any time these types of goals can be accomplished in your family will work.

2. *Set a time limit on the length of the meeting in advance and keep your agreement.* Usually thirty minutes to an hour is best in the beginning. Let one member be the moderator at each meeting and another be the timekeeper. Some families keep notes on what is discussed. Each of these functions should be rotated regularly.

I usually suggest to the families that I work with that the youngest member be the moderator for the first session. This works for two reasons: First, that child will probably take the responsibility seriously and make sure the family actually gets together. Second, in many families it will allow Dad not to be the first one to speak, and perhaps dominate the conversation.

3. *Each member of the family gets the opportunity to say what he or she thinks without being interrupted by another family member.* How do you do that? One gimmick is the use of a timer that can be passed from one member to the next as his turn to speak comes. Each person has an allotted time to comment on an issue before other members respond. Another helpful rule is that no member should speak twice on an issue until all the family members have had an opportunity to speak at least once.

4. *Treat each member's feelings or ideas equally in the family meeting.* All may not have equal authority, but each should be given a respectful hearing in the family meetings. Letting your children feel that they can honestly express their feelings and frustrations toward all the members of the family will not erode your authority. I know this works, because I have made it a rule that a child can share any feeling in my office, and the parents agree not to punish the child for what

is said. I ask if anything said made a difference in the time between sessions. Children are honest enough to tell me, and parents report a sense of relief at not having to correct whatever "bad impressions" I might get about the family because of what the children said.

5. *Between meetings of the family, use a storage area for the problems to be addressed in the coming meeting.* One family I worked with created what the kids called a "gripe pipe." It was made of three metal soft-drink cans taped together. Complaints were written and stored in the pipe, to be read and discussed at the next session.

What this accomplished was some dumping onto paper of the issues that had been sources of bitterness in previous times. Obviously a shoe box or a card file will work equally well. The way you collect the issues is less important than the fact that your family meets to talk face-to-face. The single most important place to learn that your ideas and feelings count is in your home. I believe that what happens in your family can effect change in the community. If our children learn to communicate at home, perhaps that strength will change the way they function internationally in a coming decade.

Being an effective communicator improves every dimension of living, but it is essential in the close arena of the family. Having seen more than 7,000 couples in the course of my practice, I have become familiar with the most common complaint between people—"lack of communication." That is the chief source of difficulty in the family today.

The issue is not, however, the lack of speech or conversation. We do communicate in many ways that we are not aware of. The key is to improve the skills of the entire family to facilitate clear communication, providing the building blocks of good relationships.

Whether each member of the family learns individually or we engage in joint family therapy, there are two essential skills to which we must be introduced: self-disclosure and reflection. Bringing about change in the family relationship begins with strategic intervention in the communication process.

Mert and Patricia and their two sons, Carl and Kevin, came into my office a few years ago. Carl, the sixteen-year-old, was the identified patient. He had been acting unusually depressed and talking about suicide. I agreed to see only the entire family, in order to demonstrate that the problems of a sixteen-year-old do not exist in isolation.

Having spent some individual time with each member of the family and evaluating a set of psychological inventories with the family group, we agreed on a treatment plan to be followed. Our goal was to change the family system so that Carl no longer carried so much of the negative emotion within the family interaction.

To do that meant that each member of the family had to be very clear about the concept of feeling responsibility. I introduced them to the idea that no one else can be aware of or respond to my feelings until I accept the responsibility for communicating them clearly. The first law of communication is simply stated: I am responsible for my feelings, thoughts, words, and actions. No one else can usurp that position. I cannot blame someone else for the way I feel, think, speak, or act.

The second law of communication is equally important: Before I respond to what another person has said to me, I replay to him what I heard. Otherwise, the communication will often be about something I perceived, which may be different from what the other person thought he said.

To practice these rules and to lay the foundation for

clearer communication, we did some exercises demonstrating self-disclosure and reflection. In order to participate, each member of the family had to begin any sentence with the word *I* in order to speak. He could follow that with *feel, think, sense,* or *want.* It took a while and several interruptions before the blaming pattern characterized by starting sentences with *you* was interrupted.

Try tape recording an hour or so of conversation in your home. What you'll discover is that a number of misunderstandings occur when a member of the family feels blamed or accused by another. A typical vignette goes like this:

"You ought to know better than that——."

"I suppose you could have done better——."

Another blaming sentence begins, "You make me mad——."

And the response defensively comes back, "I didn't do anything. You——."

These kinds of conversations are so common I am sure you can fill in the blanks.

If you don't want to acknowledge these types of conversations in your home, you can use the technique I offer audiences when I lecture publicly and a question-and-answer period follows. You may begin your question with, "My neighbor has this problem," or "My aunt and uncle fought about——." If it's more comfortable, think about the way the conversations went in the home you grew up in or how it sounds at a neighbor's household. Then you can focus on your own situation.

The Mortons—Mert, Patricia, Carl, and Kevin—were good people to have in therapy. They didn't like coming to my office at first, but they soon got into the sessions and began to get some real insights about themselves. After a particularly difficult confrontation with his father, Carl said,

"I used to think I wanted to die, but now I think Dad and I might even become friends—maybe." The family system had begun to change. This family was learning how to express love for one another.

Another communication-skill builder this family used to embody the self-disclosure and reflection process is the L-O-V-E acrostic. LOVE is a four-act communication drama. These are the four acts:

L is for listening "Listening is the profound activity of silent love," reads one of my favorite posters. In our busy and hectic world, one of the most priceless of gifts is that of attention. If you really care about someone, you take the time to hear what he says. It is all too easy to miss what is being said.

A minister friend of mine says that when he was the preaching pastor in a large church, he was preoccupied with something while he shook hands with parishioners at the back of the church following Sunday worship. He was making the usual, "Good morning. God bless you" comments when he realized that, several handshakes before, a member of the congregation had told him he was experiencing a personal crisis. It may be an apocryphal story, but I can certainly recall times when I have been caught up in my own thoughts and missed chunks of conversation. Unfortunately, some of those occasions were at home. Listening really provides the foundation for loving experiences. We can avoid listening in order not to feel pain, or we can miss the opportunity to share the joy of another by simply failing to listen.

O is for observing Caring, especially in the family, means seeing as well as hearing what another person communicates to you. Use your eyes to pick up on nonverbal gestures or the situational elements. That way, you see the whole picture of the message, rather than just hearing the words.

Two dear friends, Denny and Varian Spear of Dunwoody, Georgia, work with marriage enrichment groups. Recently they demonstrated to the assembled couples in the room the way their marital communication used to be. Standing back to back, they intertwined their arms and talked to each other. They were touching, but neither could see the expressions on the other's face. Finally, they turned and faced each other, and both smiled. It was a classic illustration of the value of observation.

The look of love may well be the concentration we give to another's facial and body language when we communicate. The message is: Watch what other people say to you.

V is for verifying The art of reflection comes into play here. The simple repetition of what another has said can save a good deal of time and energy in communicating. I've watched hundreds of family members argue over a mistaken message. The use of a clarifying question such as, "Is this what you meant? If I heard you right, you said . . ." is a useful response. These easily learned techniques help us to understand what the ones we love want to communicate to us.

Reflective contact keeps us from responding to the wrong part of something another person says. In the seventh or eighth session I had with a certain couple, the husband reluctantly but sincerely began their hour by saying, "Doctor, my wife is the stubbornest woman in the world. She insisted we came to counseling. If it hadn't been for her, we would not be here, and things wouldn't be as good in our marriage as they are today. I have to admire her for helping us to improve."

When he stopped speaking, his wife almost exploded from her chair with, "Do I have to listen to this kind of stuff again today?" She was fuming.

I asked her what she heard her husband say, and she responded, "He said I was the stubbornest woman in the world!" When I asked if she heard anything else, she said, "He didn't say much else." I repeated what I thought he had said to me. "He didn't say that!" Finally, since on that occasion I had a tape recorder going, I played back what he had said, and she said, "Did he really say that?" The problem was that she heard only the first part and then began thinking about her response. She was watching his lips to see when he would stop speaking so that she could tell him how angry she was. Too often we observe but don't verify, and the communication goes awry.

Verifying helps us to be sure that we listened and observed correctly. It also affirms that the other person did communicate what he intended to say.

E is for enriching We enhance each other with two-way communication. We parents find it too easy to forget that listening to our children is as important as talking to them. Listening and responding enrich the process of talking to those we love. Loving communication links us together.

I imagine so many family interactions as being like two television sets turned toward each other, both broadcasting their information, but neither receiving anything useful in the process! Family communication needs to include working receivers and transmitters. This mutual process improves both sides of the communication.

The language of family love is multidimensional, verbal and nonverbal. Giving the gift of effective communication can produce priceless emotional dividends.

PART FOUR

Parenting Profits

THE PARENT'S CREED
If a child lives with criticism,
    He learns to condemn.
If a child lives with hostility,
    He learns to fight.
If a child lives with ridicule,
    He learns to be shy.
If a child lives with shame,
    He learns to feel guilty.
If a child lives with tolerance,
    He learns to be patient.
If a child lives with encouragement,
    He learns confidence.
If a child lives with praise,
    He learns to appreciate.
If a child lives with fairness,
    He learns justice.
If a child lives with security,
    He learns to have faith.
If a child lives with approval,
    He learns to like himself.
If a child lives with acceptance and
   friendship,
    He learns to find love in the world.
               Dorothy Law Nolte

THIRTEEN

The Friends Who Once Were Children

> If you give a man a fish,
> you feed him for a day;
> If you teach a man how to fish,
> you feed him for life.
> **Chinese Proverb**

Harry Chapin's song "Cat's in the Cradle" is not only musically imaginative, but has struck deeply into many parents' hearts, both positively and negatively. The promises for good times in the future never came for the son, or for the father later. Yet most of us have dreams about the future of our families and our relationships with our children. What will they be like?

I hear many guilty confessions like this: "I hate to admit it, but I don't like my mother [or father]. I live less than five miles away. I find excuses not to go by. I resent being expected to come for Sunday lunch so often." Well over a hundred adults have complained to me about their relationships with their parents. As I've discussed it with them, I think I've learned an important principle: We only spend as much time with our parents, with the exception of family holidays, as we would with any other adult we like. Once childhood is over, friendship must be the driving force in the relationship between adult parents and adult children.

You'll recognize that there are some nonadult parents. Those are the demanding and manipulative types who constantly blame their adult children for their lack of contact. Instead of being glad their grown child called, this parent chides him for failing to call sooner. Or, forgetting that the child may have something to share, the parent recites his own problems, ailments, or interests. Is it any wonder that the grown child calls infrequently?

The other type of problem in this relationship is the nonadult child. He refuses to grow up and accept responsibility for himself. He expects continual parental care, professing independence but demanding either financial or emotional support on an ongoing basis. It's tough for the parent of such a child not to wish he could, as one father put it, "run away from home."

I have never met a child to whom his parents were unimportant, even when they were unknown. The search for our origins is based in the kind of parents our heritage holds, and then in the environment which they largely shaped for us. The sense of knowing who I am often arises from knowing who they are (or were). The renewed interest in genealogy reinforces this view. Two of my patients illustrate our need to accept our origins.

Jack is a somewhat frantic and angry young man, still struggling with his interrupted—and perhaps postponed— adolescence. He recalls his parents as being strict and somewhat verbally abusive. Like so many sons who feel driven, Jack could not remember his father touching him or saying that he loved him. That is a contributing factor to Jack's exaggerated needs in marriage. He is insanely jealous of his wife and excessively demanding on his own children, even to the point of physically punishing them. His outbursts have resulted in physical attacks on his wife. She has been vulnerable to the comfort and consolation of other men, which is not the central issue of this discussion.

Jack's need for his parents' acceptance still drives him. His chosen career not only reflects some talent, but also indicates his great need for recognition and acceptance. Now that Jack is chronologically an adult, he avoids his parents, even at holidays. "They didn't like me, and I don't need them. My old man cursed me when I was a kid. I won't give him that chance again." Yet in Jack's more reflective moments, the tears well up in his eyes as he speaks about childhood disappointments in the family. Jack's case is extreme but illustrative.

Cheryl had a similar problem with her past. Being a first child, she had a stronger-than-average need to be accepted and praised by her parents. Older brothers and sisters can sometimes provide some of that comfort and reassurance for the younger children, but the oldest child stands alone. Cheryl's parents became Christians when she was in grade school. The change in their lives was not drastic, but was meaningful. Her mother had an intense interest in bringing Cheryl to her newly discovered faith. Because her mother was by nature manipulative, Cheryl responded, but she felt controlled and never good enough to meet her mother's expectations. Because this occurred at the onset of puberty, much of Cheryl's later rebellion took on sexual overtones. Her marriages failed; she saw herself as a flagrant violator of sexual mores and felt condemned before God. She tried so hard with her own children, but felt overwhelmed and "like a colossal failure, even though my kids are the most important thing in the world to me."

I am convinced that both Jack's and Cheryl's parents intended to be good role models and to provide a solid home foundation that would lead to good relationships in later life. Having had some sessions with older parents like them, I know some of the disappointments they feel at this stage of their lives. I raised a question in chapter one: What are the things you can do today to insure successful parenting forty years from now? It's time to address that issue.

To bring your children to adulthood and still have your own mental health intact, there are two emphases which must run through the process: firmness and fairness.

Firmness

We've talked about love, which is the foundation of firmness with our children. Our own self-confidence is another building block in the firmness pattern. But firmness is not based on hostile or belittling restrictions on our children. We first need to resolve some of the messages we are still carrying around from our own parents.

Transactional analysis has developed some ideas about the parent within ourselves. A helpful book is *Your Inner Child of the Past*, by W. Hugh Missildine. Both sources recommend understanding your own experiences and gaining the ability to "parent" yourself inwardly. Reread the initial chapters of this book, about examining your own past and the questions useful to that process. Then ask yourself what conclusions you have reached about your ability to parent. Most of us have developed some irrational thoughts that we don't acknowledge.

Jack believes that, although he loves his children, his own model for being a parent is so poor that he must leave his children, for fear of ruining their lives. His limited interpretation of the possibilities of the past contributes to his desire to escape the responsibilities of parenting.

Firmness is self-centered, as well as child oriented. It's

sometimes necessary to have some conversations with ourselves—or perhaps with a qualified family therapist—to begin to reshape our confidence in being successful parents. I reminded Jack that he knew what he did *not* want in the relationship with his children. As he thought through the mistakes his parents made, we began to list some of the goals *he* had. Writing down your parental goals helps you think about them and reinforces them in your mind. Out of our conversations, three goals emerged: time, talk, and trust.

The firm parent takes time. Jack said, "My father never had time for me. He was always so preoccupied with other things." The commitment to parenting involves the time to think about your needs and to be involved with your child's needs. Children ask good questions, if we allow them.

Jack and I had a good laugh over the story of the little boy who asked his father, "Dad, who made God?"

The father, without looking up from the evening newspaper, said, "I don't know, Son."

The little guy continued, "Why is the earth round?"

Dad answered, "Beats me."

After playing for a few minutes more, the little boy asked, "Dad, is there life on other planets?"

The father patiently answered, "Nobody knows the answer to that question."

Finally, the little boy said, "Dad, do you mind me asking you all these questions?"

The father looked over his paper and said, "Why, not at all, Son. How else are you going to learn anything?"

Time may only be the willingness to listen and to try to explain the unexplainable to a child. But your giving time is a statement of your child's value to you, as compared to other things in life. The effective parent may not know all the answers, but he takes the time to listen to the questions and may seek the answers with the child.

Time may be most important in the area of discipline. Cheryl cited many examples where she thought she was punished not for what she had done, but for the person she was. Her mother, perhaps without knowing it, gave her the message that she was unloved and unwanted. Time is essential to explain the rules and guidelines of the family. Good discipline reflects a previous conversation or principle that a parent has made clear to his child, rather than a surprise response to a disappointing deed.

The family conference can be a great use of time, not only for clarifying expectations but for reaching new understandings of situations or problems. Neither Cheryl nor Jack could remember a time when their parents sat down with them and explained their goals for the family or their ideas about parenting. The parent who knows his own ideas and is willing to be firm in his expectations allows for questions and discussion but still reserves the right to make final decisions. The family conference is not a democratic election; as a parent, you may still overrule objections or dissensions. The key is that you take the time to give your child a hearing.

The firm parent talks. The effective parent will not hide behind his authority. He will use his authority to explain why he has established the rules and regulations that are in effect in the home. If the parents disagree about the rules, their discrepancies should be worked out for the most part in private, and their presentation to the children should be unified. I rarely say *never* or *always*, but I believe that it is *always* harmful to a child when parents are divided and side with a child against each other. The only exception would be in a situation concerning the physical safety of the child. Otherwise, the rule is, *never* agree with your child and oppose your spouse. Take the time to talk over the differences in your point of view and even explain them to the children together.

This insistent position grows out of the conclusions reached from the work of Bowlby. He demonstrated that children who are patients improved when they saw their parents as being closer to each other than either of them was to the child. The children did not improve with treatment when they perceived themselves as closer to one of the parents than the parents were to each other. In short, the child develops with security on the strong foundation of the marital commitment. The absence of that strength weakens the child's position and causes him to question his own value. This raises serious questions about the impact of divorce on a child.

A corrective must be mentioned. Where one parent is forced, by whatever circumstances, to rear the child alone, the result is not automatically negative, but it requires much more time and talk for understanding and security to be achieved.

The value of talking and listening to your child cannot be overestimated. I grew up in a Georgia home, of which I am proud, but the predominant philosophy among parents was "Children should be seen and not heard." When that axiom is fully carried out, the child often gets a message of discounted value. Women's liberation has in part been a reaction to the role of being seen and not heard at a number of levels in our society. Could it be that some of our children's rebellions have also been based on a sense of being devalued? The result is often a frontal attack on the things the parents seem to value most. Could that be in part an explanation for why the children of religious parents often seem to rebel against their parents' faith?

I'm not suggesting for a moment that all adult conversation should be interrupted, set aside, or dominated by the verbalization of a child. That would give vent to another extreme—the child-dominated home. That kind of home almost always ends in disaster for both children and parents. Listening to our children in private and in public confirms their sense of worth and their meaningful participation in life. Nothing says how important another person is as much as the gift of attention. When we fail to pay attention to them, are we protecting ourselves from what they might say that would reflect poorly on us?

Art Linkletter used to ask children, "What was it that your parents told you not to say on television today?" Invariably the innocent child would volunteer the taboo subject, to the roar of the audience. A poster I have kept for several years reads, "Listening is the profound activity of silent love." Try to find a special time to listen to your child, and perhaps some new ways to begin to introduce him to adult conversations.

A little boy sitting with his parents at a restaurant was asked, "What would you like to eat?"

"A hot dog and a soda," he gleefully replied.

"He'll have a glass of milk and a bowl of soup," his mother said.

"One soda and hot dog coming up," the waitress said.

As she walked away, the little guy said to his mother, "Gee, Mommy, she thinks I'm real." Listening does convey a sense of value.

Talking is a two-way process. When you listen to your child, you'll know what he needs to hear. You will also find that some conversations are unnecessary. One of our most difficult areas is that of sex education. Many of us have laughed at the story of the mother whose son came in from playing to ask, "Where did I come from?"

She knew he would eventually ask about sex, so she patiently explained the birds and the bees and how children were born. "Do you understand now, Johnny?" she asked.

"I guess so, Mom," said Johnny. "Billy said he came from Detroit, and I just wanted to know where I came from."

We've learned so much and prepared ourselves to share with our children, but we need to let them guide us in the amount of information we share.

A parent can never go wrong if he talks about his love for his child and shares his own feelings about any situation. You are the expert on you and your feelings. No one can deny that. What we call "*I* messages," meaning sentences that begin *I feel, I think, I sense,* and so forth, are always appropriate for parents. What follows will be something you can accept the responsibility for in your conversations.

Let me return to Cheryl for a moment. In her conversations with her mother, there was a good deal of talking, but it was mostly her mother telling Cheryl what the Bible commanded her to do. Cheryl began to feel that any disagreement she had with her mother was a difference of opinion with God. She began to keep more and more things inside her. She talked less to her mother, and by the time she was a teenager, she was tolerating her mother's "preaching." Cheryl has, of course, exaggerated her mother's behavior, but the focal point is probably accurate. How can you overcome the danger of talking too much? Balance it with listening. Listen as much as you talk, and then listen a little more. That will lead to the third mark of a firm parent: trust.

The firm parent trusts.   Trust implies honesty, dependence on each other, and faith in what is shared. Perhaps the key to trust is the refusal to judge inappropriately or harshly. When I trust someone, I believe in his intent to help, not harm me. A parent must believe in his commitment to his children and then convey that sense of acceptance to them.

Trust means that no questions are off limits. Certainly some discussions are better held in private than in public. All a parent has to do when a difficult question is raised in public is to acknowledge the query and agree to discuss it later, when the two of you are alone. Trust is the arena in which good communication is fostered.

Have you ever noticed how some families seem to be comfortable talking about any issue? Other families seem to "freeze" when subjects that are unpleasant or unfamiliar arise in conversation.

Not long ago I consulted with a parent-school organization about an upsetting problem. One young boy had been referred to my office because of "emotional problems." As I got to know the child, I discovered that he and his parents lived in a rural area, where the open atmosphere in the family made it easy for him to learn about both animal and human reproductive systems. When he shared this information with other children at his school, and they rather innocently told their parents, some of the parents were upset by what their children knew.

The biggest problems we face in our families are not caused by what we know, but rather by what we do not know or do not say. Strong families can openly discuss any issue, sometimes seriously and often humorously, without embarrassment. Be thankful if your children talk to you, and take a bow if they listen! You have a strong parent-child relationship. Here are a few tips for talking.

1. *Say what you feel, as well as what you think, when you talk.* Fathers especially need to be reminded that the heart says some things so much better than the head. Loving words sometimes make more sense than logic does. Never be afraid to tell a member of your family how you feel. Your attitudes have probably already registered with them, and they will feel better that you have admitted what their senses are picking up.

2. *Separate people and behavior when you talk.* Mother's action may be miserable, but she isn't. Tell your child you don't like what he said or did, but that you still love him. The single most important distinction one can make in talking to others is to know the difference between what people do and who they are.

3. *Speak specifically; don't generalize.* This is especially true in criticism. Your children don't *always* or *never* do anything. Those generalizations often hurt and humiliate. They are blaming responses. Avoid them and improve your corrections.

Fairness

When you exhibit the spirit of fairness in your parenting, it is easier to move on to difficult areas in the relationship. Fairness in the family is not democracy in terms of one person, one vote. You as the parents have the responsibility and set the rules. You hold the power. Successful parents use their power more effectively than parents who fail.

Why do most families experience misunderstandings and hard feelings? The answer is so simple that it is easily overlooked: They don't talk to one another. Communication is the secret to family peace.

I only dare parents to do three things: discipline, discuss, and disclose. Accept the responsibility for setting the limits. Administer those limits with a sense of fairness and openness of style. Discuss your child's needs and objections. Listen carefully. Take time to consider their objections, and then tell them the decision you've reached. Finally, disclose yourself to your children. It will help you as much as it does them. The more I share of me in a trusting way with my child, the more I will learn of myself. I will be more predictable to my child and give him more security in the relationship. That will be the basis for an ongoing friendship between us in the future.

A final word on the friends who once were your children. They emerge from a good relationship over the years, but they deserve the same consideration new friends would get. Don't assume actions on the part of your children. I wouldn't dare speak for a friend by saying, "He'll be glad to do that," yet I have heard parents make those kinds of commitments for their children. Ask them. Invite them to share, but don't presume the right to decide for them. You'll be better friends for years to come.

FOURTEEN

Renewing the Postparental Marriage

"Love does not dominate; it cultivates."

Goethe

Having seen a lot of marriages, I don't get too many surprises; but an increasing trend in the last few years has troubled me—the breakup of the postparental marriage. Marriages of twenty to forty years duration are being severed in the divorce courts too frequently. The issue is certainly complicated, but one of the causes is the failure to renew the marriage after the children leave home.

The ideal marriage is one that begins with a strong bond of commitment, develops more intimacy and depth during the prechild years, adds growth while the children are home, and then enjoys the more relaxed and less hectic years after the children are adults. If you are just at the beginning stages of parenthood, make that experience your aim. Too many couples fall short.

Frank was a troubled man when he slumped into the chair in my office. He looked the part of the executive, but in his face the etchings of time were clearly present. I judged him to be close to retirement age and was surprised to find that he was only fifty-six. He was a deliberate southern gentleman who had difficulty admitting his problem. Finally he said, "I'd like to have my wife back, but it may be too late."

The rest of the story was too familiar. Frank had busied himself with making a living, while Marilyn had stayed home with the children. Some pregnancy problems, some lack of consideration on his part for the load she was carrying at home, and a lot of years with nothing but functional communication had left her devoid of romantic feelings. She announced one day that she would prefer separate bedrooms for the duration of the marriage. Although there had been little tenderness and minimal love talk, they had still engaged in their every-other Tuesday night sexual intercourse for the last decade. While Frank professed to be sexually faithful, he admitted he occasionally had dinner with a woman associate when he traveled. "I need someone to talk to . . . sometime," he protested.

The last of their three daughters had married and left home two years earlier, and now Marilyn had found a part-time job. She was much more happy about that than about her relationship with Frank. "Especially when he comes home drunk. All he needs is a female body," she said angrily, after she had joined the sessions later.

With some modifications, their story represents a common complaint. During the parenting years, he has spent more time devoting himself to his job, and she has devoted herself to her job of being with the children. When the children are gone, there are no more satisfactory personal feelings to draw them to each other. Now that they have no children in common, the purpose for the marriage seems gone.

Olga and Stan were different. They knew they were in trouble several years before she resumed her career in the travel agency. They had a decent physical relationship, but the emotional closeness and any sense of spiritual sharing were missing. Through a college friend, their daughter had encouraged them to come to see me. "We don't plan to get a divorce," he said.

When I asked them if they had a plan for the next twenty-five years of their lives, she looked hurt. "We made it through the first twenty-five—I guess we'll survive the next twenty-five, too," she joked.

I got them to talk about the beginning years of their marriage, their early happiness, and their dreams for the future. After our first session and two individual meetings, we looked at some psychological inventories, which revealed a great deal of similarity between them. One of the dangers of such a marriage is that it can be boring and predictable, so we planned some new adventures for them as a couple. They took an evening course at college together; they developed a new winter hobby for the indoor months. They took up sailing for the warmer months and bought their first boat, something they had talked about for years but felt they couldn't afford as long as they had children to support.

We talked about some of their financial planning. Stan had not thought seriously about retiring early, but Olga's eyes brightened as I asked him about the possibilities. "We could be free to travel so much more," she said, excitedly. He explored some of the options and discovered a satisfying way to leave the company early. The net result was two people who became stimulated about sharing plans with each other and developed a new sense of direction in their relationship. Marriage is, after all, not as much two people gazing into each other's eyes romantically as it is two people standing shoulder to shoulder, sharing the same goal.

Renewal of the postparental marriage is based on some fairly specific steps. If you are at that stage, try these on for size:

1. *Review the past relationship and identify the joys and satisfactions you have shared together, especially before the children came.* Find the ways each of you has contributed to the other's life, and express appreciation for those. Positive reinforcement of the early attractions and successes of the marriage is essential to this renewal process.

2. *Recognize and utilize the basic laws of change in relationship.* The laws are: I can only change myself. I cannot change you. If I change, you have to change in relationship to me. Those sound so simple, but their effect can be profound when practiced. When I take charge of a problem through the part I can control, things begin to change. When my happiness depends on the actions or attitudes of another, I will always be unhappy. When I do what I can, I feel better, because I am being responsible. Two responsible people can bring about significant change in their marriage by a common vision and cooperative effort.

3. *Expect results and things happen.* If you feel it's "too late," you are already defeated. The philosopher Seneca said, "Madness is to be expecting evil before it comes." If that's true, then perhaps the definition of sanity is to be expecting the positive. The most mentally healthy people I know expect good results, and they usually get them. I stood near a casket with a widow some years ago—just the two of us. She whispered toward the casket, "I wish I had told you I loved

you more often." That's too late, but as long as you and your spouse are breathing, there's the possibiity of change and renewal in the relationship.

George Bernard Shaw's words have been used in many situations. I think these words of his apply very specifically to the years after our children leave us, "You see things as they are and ask, Why? But I dream things that never were and ask, Why not?"

The empty nest can be filled with laughter and pleasure—the joys of new discoveries together. Why not?

FIFTEEN

Maintaining Your Mental Health While Your Children Grow Up

> The man who knows right from wrong and has good judgment and common sense is happier than the man who is immensely rich! For such wisdom is far more valuable than precious jewels. Nothing else compares with it.
>
> **Proverbs 3:13–15** TLB

In my weekly newspaper column, I wrote some ideas about "the unpardonable parental error." I intended parents to ask themselves if they were giving their children what was most important in life. The column grew out of this encounter in my office.

"I think I've ruined my daughter's life." The mother spoke through tight lips and with a grim expression. She told me her story, and I was able to reassure her that she had not made an irreversible mistake in dealing with her daughter. But she caused me to think about that question. Is there an unpardonable error that a parent can make?

I have several hundred posters in my collection. One of my favorites says: "The greatest gift one can give another is a deeper understanding of life and the ability to love and believe in himself." That sums up the essence of the parental responsibility: to give your child a deep understanding of life and the ability to believe in and love himself.

My personal conviction is that one cannot believe in himself until he understands that God loves and accepts him. A full parental education of a child will include sharing the deeper spiritual values of life. That is the complete process of the deeper understanding and inviting your child to become excited about his place in life.

Family traditions are often among the most lasting memories of our childhood. Many of them center around the special holidays in the calendar year. Easter Sunday is a great family day, as well as the greatest event on the church calendar.

Along with the gift baskets and Easter egg hunts, we usually have new clothes and some good feelings about the coming of spring and the anticipation of flowers and outdoor activities. Too many families miss the opportunity for a most significant teaching time for children and the gift of hope to the next generation.

The resurrection of Jesus reminds us that life's seeming defeats can be turned into victory. Even those who are not believers can find the element of hope in the Gospel story. For those who believe, the Easter experience provides an all-important sharing time in the family. Every family has been touched by grief and sorrow. The promise of Jesus,

"Because I live, you too shall live," offers families a promised reunion in the future. Hope may be the greatest force for mental stability in an individual, and the loss of hope is a critical deficit in a person's mental health.

While I was in graduate school, a learned professor ridiculed the miracles of the New Testament, including the resurrection of Jesus. When he finished, I told him I had a funeral to attend the next day. "If I accept your philosophy of life and don't have the promise of a resurrection to offer the grieving family, what do you have to offer in its place?" He was silent for a moment and then replied, "Nothing." I told him that until I was convinced of something superior to faith in the resurrection, I would keep offering that hope to families facing the crisis of death. When I talk to parents about values, I emphasize that that's one of the questions each of us must ask himself: "If I don't give my children my faith in the resurrection, what will I give them as a basis of hope for their future?"

It borders on an unpardonable error for a parent not to share his values with his child. Much of his self-esteem will be based not only on how he feels about himself, but also on what he has decided are his values for living. The methodology for teaching values is basically simple. Here are three suggestions I have shared with parents:

1.   *Tell your child every day that you love him because of who he is and not on the basis of what he does.* True love is unconditional. Don't say "I'll love you if. . . ." (And that includes "I'll love you if you believe as I do.") Conditional love is forever unattainable to a child. Share your values because they are important to you, and your child will respect them and try them on for size.

2.   *Show your child your values by modeling them.* Touch him and physically express affection every day. The absence of

expressed parental affection, verbal and nonverbal, is one of the most common complaints of the people I see in family counseling. "I didn't learn how to be comfortable with physical affection, because we didn't do that in our home." That's a typical response.

3. *Learn to praise your child's successes, and encourage him to correct his mistakes.* He will come to trust you and ask for your help, whatever his age. If you ignore his faults, he will know you don't take him seriously.

The parent who honestly shares himself and reaches out to his child will not be guilty of robbing that child of the most precious of gifts—the ability to believe in himself and to have a deeper understanding of life.

Losing Your Mental Health

Very few parents actually go crazy in the process of rearing children, but too many act in strange ways that are irrational. The justification for this behavior is based on some notion that parents are supposed to sacrifice themselves for their children. Indeed, that may be the unpardonable parental error. It is not a failure in the responsibility toward the child, but a tragic loss of perspective about one's own value in the process of helping the child grow up.

Children who grow up with parents who irrationally accept the sacrificial role pass that on to their children. We become carriers of unhealthy emotional attitudes. The rest of this book might well center around this key concept: Don't lose your mental health helping your children grow up.

Parenting, despite its burdens and challenges, still provides us with a wealth of memories, the majority of which can be happy. But I want to see a new generation of parents who have good memories about their children growing up, along with some good feelings about their careers, accomplishments, and marriages, too.

Love your child, but don't lose yourself in him. Good parenting is a process of interaction with the child, not capitulation to the child's needs and wishes.

When you write for the public, people begin to feel they know you. Most of the time, it is one of the great extras of being an author. Occasionally, someone will write who simply shares an experience without asking for advice or solution. This was one of those letters:

Dear Dr. Kilgore:

I read your columns and have read several of your books. I agree with so much of what you say, especially your ideas about family life. I hope you won't mind if I share some of my life with you.

I am seventy-six years old. I live in a nursing home now. I was married for fifty-two years. My husband died twelve years ago. We have seven children—four sons and three daughters—all of whom are married, and I have eighteen grandchildren now.

I am lonely for my children. They are good children, but they are busy. I see some of them about once a week. I do love seeing my grandchildren so.

I don't regret what I did as a parent. I love my children. I am disappointed that my children don't visit me more. I think they love me, but I'm doing now what I did when they grew up. I always put them first. I bought clothes for them when I needed a new dress or Dad needed a new pair of shoes. Yesterday one of my sons came for his monthly visit. I've never seen his home; I'd like to. I don't drive anymore, but some friends from a nearby church and one of my daughters do take me out to the doctor's office or for lunch on special occasions.

There's nothing you can do for me, but tell those young parents you help to do something different than I did. I don't like feeling hurt or bitter, and most of the time I go around to visit those people here who have no relatives or children to see them. It makes me feel better. There must be a better way to raise children than I did. I guess if you let them take you for granted while they are growing up, they can take you for granted when you don't have too many years left.

Thank you for reading this.

When I first read that letter, I felt some pity for the author. As I thought about it later, I felt angry toward her children. Then I began asking myself if I might someday feel that way about my life as a parent. Perhaps the key question before all parents is this: How can I be a whole person, live a full life, and still be responsible in the way I rear my children? The answer cannot be given apart from your understanding of how you fit into the family system. All of us would do well to grade our homelife. We need to reflect on the home in which we grew up, to understand our background, but we need to examine our present homes to see where we fit into the pattern of our immediate living.

The other day I saw a teacher filling out progress reports on her students for the quarter. In the mail that day I received a survey requesting my evaluation of the automobile I had purchased about a year earlier. We are asked to evaluate or grade many products and services, but I can't recall being asked to assess my family life or home situation outside a therapy setting. Let's grade our homelives today.

Is your family a nice place to live? Are you happy to be a

member of the group you call a family? What would you change about your family, if you had the power to do so? All of those are the usual kinds of questions one might ask to evaluate a product or service. Here are some specifics to apply to your family:

1. *What is the greatest strength I contribute to my family?* I asked a family with two teenagers that question, and the younger son said, "I keep things loose in my family." They all laughed, but he had *demonstrated* one of his strengths—his sense of humor. When things get tense, he helps his family cope by seeing the lighter side of the issue. Obviously, humor can be distracting at times, but it also helps in many of the difficult circumstances of homelife. As you look at your home, what strength or assets do you add to the family system?

2. *What do I do to keep my family positive?* A father brought his teenager to therapy and discovered in a family session that he was perceived as the most negative member of the family. The youngest said, "Dad is so grouchy!" In a relatively short time, that father began to change his approach, and the teenager responded quickly. Try taking a piece of paper and listing the things you do to make your family atmosphere positive.

3. *What role do I play in the family drama?* Every family has a script, even if unacknowledged. Am I a leader or a follower in my family? Do I start the arguments or work toward a reconciliation? Do I cheerfully share the load of maintaining the family needs, or am I a griper and complainer about the responsibilities I have?

Well, what's your grade going to be? The healthy parent is the one who knows himself so well that few things his children tell him will come as a surprise, even if they are criticisms. My goal as a healthy person is to know myself so well that I won't have to fear any feedback from a friend or an enemy. Surely children fall somewhere in between those extremes.

The essential ingredients for maintaining one's mental health as a parent don't vary much from the general requirements. There are four necessities to emotional balance in my life: awareness, honesty, trust, and freedom. These must be practiced across parental responsibility, career lines, community involvement, and personal growth. These are the key parts of self-actualization for the parent. The more I understand and practice these four areas of psychological reality, the more likely I am to be a success at parenting.

Awareness

Awareness is the initial step of self-understanding. Thinking through my needs and feeling comfortable with my knowledge of myself is vital to all my relationships. Parenting is a personal relationship rather than a task. As such, the parent demands of himself an introspection that creates his own bank of information and inspiration to be shared with his child. Words that express that awareness are important, but the senses are so much more important. What I *feel* needs to be shared, as well as what I *know*. I teach through my limitations as well as through my strengths.

In a postdoctoral training program, I was teamed up with a blind therapist for a couples' group treatment program. Together, my cotherapist, the group, and I learned how to use his blindness as an asset to our experience. I had husbands and wives describe their spouses to him. He in turn sometimes heard things differently from the way others in the group saw them. This experience reminded me of pa.ents

144

who seem to apologize for their handicaps or those of their children, rather than maximizing them as an unexplored asset for greater awareness. As I am courageous enough to look into the unknown about myself, not only do I grow, but my children benefit, because I have more of me accessible for sharing with them. That's not psychological selling; it's reality for me and many parents with whom I have worked.

Honesty

The second essential for maintaining my mental health is honesty. In the family relationship, parents gain miles of leadership position when they are honest enough to admit to their children that they do not know something. That is so difficult to practice, because we all fear being seen as failures. That fear makes the vulnerability of saying "I don't know" even more terrifying, until we discover that people respect our honesty.

I learned something about honesty through an early patient in sexual therapy. She brought a problem I had read about, but up to that point had not treated in my practice. I told her I thought I could help, but we got nowhere until I referred her to a well-qualified colleague who was successful in helping her deal with the problem. She became a good friend and later confided to me her appreciation for the referral. But she said, "I would have respected you even more if you had simply said to me, 'I don't have any experience with your problem,' and referred me immediately." It helped me in the future.

I'm sure I've made the same kind of mistake in fear with my children. I've observed the bravado that covers fear when parents deal with their children in therapy. Honesty is the gate through which progress is made.

Trust

Trust means risking being yourself. That is extremely difficult in parenting, because of the models each of the marriage partners bring to the relationship—their own parents. "Good" parents become the standards against which we judge ourselves, and "ineffective" parents are reminders of what we don't want to be. The mature person is willing to risk saying to his spouse, "I am not willing to be the kind of parent you are expecting, but I am working to be the best person I can be in parenting."

It is immature to decide not to parent if we cannot meet the expectations of our spouse, or even at times of our children. Effective parents risk making mistakes by trying to be themselves through the process of rearing children.

Freedom

Freedom is the final essential. That means giving to others the rights you demand for yourself. In the family, the free person allows his other family members to make mistakes, express fears, not know answers, and fail badly at times, because his honesty with himself demands it.

Freedom is not hiding behind the cliché, "Do as I say and not as I do." Instead, I give my child the space to make his mistakes, as I made mine. I may share with him the dangers I see, but if I forbid him to explore, I probably only succeed in inviting him to rebel against my rule.

I am responsible for sharing what I know as a parent with my children. As they grow, I can no longer be responsible for their behavior. I have to let them bear their own consequences and learn from them. To love a child is to give him room enough to grow.

But being a good parent never costs me my rights and my

room to grow as a person. The balance between my role and responsibility as a parent and my personal needs and growth as an individual may be a delicate one, but it is that creative tension out of which many truly great parents emerge. I have a feeling that the great kids of the world are their children.

SIXTEEN

The Strong Family

"Family life is too intimate to be preserved by the spirit of justice. It can be sustained by a spirit of love which goes beyond justice."

Reinhold Niebuhr

Successful parents create strong families. That's our goal for ourselves and our children. What we want is the best possible relationship within our homes.

The reason for that is our own experience. More than any other institution, the family determines who we are. Therefore, as a parent, I have the opportunity to determine much of my child's future feelings and development by what I do. I also can determine some of the memories I have in my later years about the parenting process. What a legacy of happiness to take into the years of maturity!

I listened to a minister friend on the radio some time ago. He said that, among other things, he hoped his children would remember his laughter. He wanted the family memories to be happy ones. That same day, out of eight cases in my office, three of my patients wept openly about the negative memories they had of their childhood and the fearful implications those experiences might have on their own ability to effectively parent. The questions they asked could be summarized this way: What can a parent do to help create a strong family?

Let me remind you of a caution implied throughout this book—the individual parent cannot take all the responsibility for the family atmosphere. I can take the personal responsibility for my input into the family. I can be responsible for communicating my feelings, thoughts, words, and actions. I cannot be solely responsible for the total outcome. Nevertheless, I can be an important creative or change agent within my family system. Knowing my goals and clearly communicating them will keep me from futile struggles with another member of the family and will minimize the negative manipulation that such conflict usually activates.

Let me suggest four almost universal characteristics of a strong family, which may become the working agenda for a parent in his own home. Strong families have these four common ingredients:

1. They appreciate one another.
2. They communicate.
3. They share common goals.
4. They spend time together.

While there is far less research about healthy families than about sick ones, these characteristics seem to show up in most of the findings. Let's look at them as goals for parenting.

Family Appreciation

A healthy self-image rests largely on the feeling of being appreciated. Parents who appreciate each other tend to teach their children to respect others, too. Following the LOVE formula—listening, observing, verifying, and enhancing—in the communication process is foundational to creating a sense of being appreciated and respected. I doubt that any human being can be told too often that he is loved. Of course, the behavior that reaffirms those words should be consistent! Members of strong families like one another, and they say so. That is not to suggest that no conflicts exist; on the contrary, conflict is expected as a normal part of the challenge of living together. Working out the difficulty together affirms the fact that you appreciate and value the relationship. We soon learn that the more valuable a relationship is, the more we will work to keep it in good working order. Parents model that for their children and reinforce it through the formative years.

As I look backing over the building years of our family, one of the continuing treasures is the clear view of the individuality and self-expression of our children. They have changed as they have matured, but there is an unmistakable sense of personal identity in each of them. Occasionally, especially when they were teenagers, it drove me up the emotional wall, but I survived to enjoy it today.

Family Communication

Strong families talk. They talk about everything—pleasant and unpleasant. Each member of the family believes it is okay for him to share his feelings and ideas. That open line of communication contributes to the good mental health of each member of the family.

There are many frustrations in the field of family therapy, but they pale when perhaps the greatest joy emerges. Fortunately, that happy experience has come frequently in my practice—to see family members begin to talk openly and happily with one another. It is almost miraculous. You see them hostile, closed, abrupt, and professing not to like one another in the early interviews. As the process begins to work, they begin to share, laugh, respond, and smile. No family portrait is more rewarding than that.

That happiness results from talking. That solution is so simple we tend to overlook it and want more dramatic ways to deal with our problems. Strong families have learned that when they communicate, they build a human network of support with one another. When they hurt, they turn to that resource first, rather than outside the family. When they have a happy experience to share, they come to one another to enjoy adding to the pleasure by sharing it with family members. Doubts can be run past another member of the family, and honest feedback will help to revise the view and give encouragement to move ahead on a project. The family base empowers action away from home.

Family Commitment to Common Goals

Families are stronger when they share common goals and values. The degree to which recreational, emotional, value, and spiritual goals are shared is a measure of the unity of that family. "The family that prays together stays together" has proven to be more than an adage. Bonding occurs with people who have similar interests at all levels of living, but especially in the family relationship.

I am not suggesting an authoritarian, dominant code of agreement, passed down from the parents to the children. What happens is more likely to be a parental sharing of their values and goals for the family, along with some compromising along the way. The parents do not have to surrender their values. Compromise means arriving at places in the heart where loving and living styles can rest until new growth takes place—together! Merely repeating my values regularly does not mean that my children will accept them as their own.

When you stop discussing things, no matter what the impasse may be, you are in a danger zone. I have not forgotten the impact of a thought I read during the Vietnam War debates: "You have not converted a man because you have silenced him." Parents building strong families stay in touch with the issues by listening to their children and by asking questions, rather than by stopping the discussion. Sharing experiences often teaches more dramatically than lecturing.

My dad is a quiet man who teaches as much by what he does not say as he does with his words. I remember the first time I wanted to get married. I was eighteen and was mature for my age, but now I know I was certainly not ready for marriage. Before I proposed, Dad suggested that he take me to a jeweler friend to look for an engagement ring. It took only a few minutes examining costly diamond rings and talking about budgets while we drove to the jewelry store to raise some serious doubts in my mind about the financial wisdom of marrying before I finished college. I chose not to propose. I don't remember my dad ever saying, "I don't think it's a good idea," but he helped me reach that decision by sharing the process nonjudgmentally. He let me learn to make my own decision, even when he was sure it was not a good one.

Parents build strong children by exposing them to the realities of life but not limiting their experiences to the parent's interpretation.

Family Activities

Strong families do things together. They share joint projects and activities and give these priority over other outside or individual interests at times. Obviously, family and individual interests have to be balanced, but the family that feels good being together can find activities to share.

Those activities change as the ages and interests of the children and parents shift. Recreational pursuits may occupy a certain period, while cultural and intellectual items may be the basic ingredient of another period.

Family decisions about activities continue the process of strong communication. One person's interests may lead the rest of the family to develop not only a curiosity but also a pursuit of that project or hobby. Dad's interest in computers may spark interest in all the members of a family. Mom's interest in tennis may get the whole family onto the courts for exercise. Competitive skills may differ, but the real goal is sharing the activity. That becomes especially crucial when athletic parents realize that their children are not only capable of winning at the games pursued, but regularly do win.

My children were all good at and interested in water sports. That influenced our decision to purchase a ski boat and eventually to live in our present home on a lake. Now that they are all grown and living their independent lives, I've learned the meaning of the two greatest days in a boat-owner's life: The second happiest is the day he buys his boat, and the happiest is the day he sells it! That ski boat did provide many hours of pleasure for our family and moments of activity we all recall when we are together now for holidays and family gatherings.

Whatever the activity, the effective parent leads the way in exploring interests and enjoying his time with the family. If you feel good being with them, they will feel good being with you. Positive reaction is a contagious feeling. Strong families enjoy doing things they like with one another.

SEVENTEEN

The Family Creed

"Discovery consists of seeing what everybody else has seen and thinking what nobody else thought."

Anonymous

The family is an institution in which we can pioneer new ideas and dimensions of life. Or we may merely evoke the memories of our past experiences by living only what those who have gone before us have taught. There is a certain entrepreneurial spirit in most of us that wants to do things our own way. The song "I Did It My Way" touches on that theme. But there is also the danger that we may try to reinvent the wheel in our attempts to be creative in the family.

I confess to no new and brilliant discoveries about the family, but it has been one of my fascinations, both personally and professionally. My conversations with family leaders in various parts of the world led me to form an organization called the International Family Foundation, Inc., which exists for the purpose of strengthening family life. Our motto is "Touch the world, one family at a time."

Back of this organization is the conviction that the family is the foundation of society. God established it so. When the family breaks apart, the world begins to crumble. The evidence is all around us.

Essentially, the family is the best hope for peace in the world. That's the message of the Family Creed:

> We believe that the family is the first and basic institution of humanity. More than any other group the family determines who we are. We want the family to be recognized, supported, and preserved in our city, nation, and world.
>
> We believe the family represents man's best hope for unity in the world. In the family all of mankind has a common bond, stronger than military, economic, educational, or political ties. The family is, therefore, the primary institution for peace in the world.
>
> We acknowledge our belief by showing love first to our own family members. We pledge respect for the rights of all those in the family of man. We want to help touch the world, one family at a time.

What we have attempted to do is to start an international dialogue with contacts through individual families. Concerned parents have responded and asked for copies of the Family Creed. We have personalized these with the last name and the member names, and they hang in several thousand homes around the world. (For more information, address your inquiry to the International Family Foundation, Inc., 1251 Marietta Highway, Canton, Georgia 30114. Phone: 404-479-3669.)

To build strong families through effective parenting and to feel good about ourselves in the process is what we are all doing. Some are more satisfied than others.

I suggest that you invite some parents you know to discuss with you the issues before all of you in your community, your church, or your neighborhood. Feeling alone as a parent limits the risks you take. Finding that you are not alone, and perhaps that other parents will stand with you to bring about change in the support systems and resources within your community, can bring great satisfaction.

What an exciting thing it would be if the next movement sweeping our country and then the world would be "parent power." Parents liberated from the permissive overlay of the last few decades would set a new tone, not only in their homes, but throughout their communities. As we reach out to one another, we can make a difference—first in our own homes, and then across the land. I could feel good about that. How about you?